200 *Fast*
chicken dishes

200 *Fast*
chicken dishes

hamlyn **all color**

An Hachette UK Company
www.hachette.co.uk

First published in Great Britain in 2015 by Hamlyn
a division of Octopus Publishing Group Ltd, Endeavour
House, 189 Shaftesbury Avenue, London, WC2H 8JY
www.octopusbooksusa.com

Distributed in the US by Hachette Book Group
1290 Avenue of the Americas, 4th and 5th Floors,
New York, NY 10020

Distributed in Canada by Canadian Manda Group,
664 Annette St., Toronto, Ontario, Canada M6S 2C8

Some of the recipes in this book have previously appeared
in other titles published by Hamlyn.

ISBN : 978-0-600-63091-3

Printed and bound in China

10 9 8 7 6 5 4 3 2 1

Standard level kitchen cup and spoon measurements
are used in all recipes.

Ovens should be preheated to the specified temperature;
if using a convection oven, follow the manufacturer's
instructions for adjusting the time and temperature.

Fresh herbs should be used unless otherwise stated.

Eggs should be large unless otherwise stated. The
U.S. Department of Agriculture advises that eggs should
not be consumed raw. This book contains dishes made with
raw or lightly cooked eggs. It is prudent for more vulnerable
people, such as pregnant and nursing mothers, people with
weakened immune systems, the elderly, babies, and young
children, to avoid uncooked or lightly cooked dishes made
with eggs. Once prepared these dishes should be kept
refrigerated and used promptly.

This book includes dishes made with nuts and nut
derivatives. It is advisable for customers with known
allergic reactions to nuts and nut derivatives and those
who may be potentially vulnerable to these allergies, such
as pregnant and nursing mothers, people with weakened
immune systems, the elderly, babies, and children, to avoid
dishes made with nuts and nut oils. It is also prudent to
check the labels of prepared ingredients for the possible
inclusion of nut derivatives.

contents

introduction   6

snacks & light bites   10

healthy feasts   52

hot & spicy   108

family favorites   154

food for friends   204

index   234

acknowledgments   240

introduction

This book offers a new and flexible approach to planning meals for busy cooks and lets you choose the recipe option that best fits the time you have available. Inside, you will find 200 dishes that will inspire you and motivate you to get cooking every day of the year.

All the recipes take a maximum of 30 minutes to cook. Some take as little as 20 minutes and, amazingly, many take only 10 minutes.

On every page, you'll find a main recipe plus a short-cut version or a fancier variation, if you have some more time on hand. Whatever you go for, you'll find a huge range of superquick recipes to get you through the week.

chicken dishes

Chicken is inexpensive, quick to cook, and immensely versatile, and its mild flavor makes it a favorite with people of every age. The unending appeal of chicken as a source of protein lies in its mild flavor, which lends itself to being blended with a host of different ingredients, from the delicate tastes of Mediterranean foods, such as basil and olives, to the rich, heavily spiced dishes of Mexico. This is why we find chicken in so many recipes from around the world, and why we have been able to include so many exciting and different recipes in this book. Think of chicken as a blank canvas to which you can add your favorite flavors. Chicken works with almost every style of cooking: Asian-style stir-fries; garlicky or herbed broiled dishes; richly spiced casseroles; warm and cold salads; Indian curries and fragrant Thai coconut recipes; French coq au vin and other wine-based stews; simple pasta dishes—the opportunities for your evening meal are almost endless.

tips and techniques

There a few simple cooking aids that really can have an amazing effect on the time spent in the kitchen.

• A food processor and a mini chopper are great time-savers.

• A good vegetable peeler and garlic press are great, simple little gadgets to help save time on otherwise fussy jobs.

• Good, sharp knives make food preparation simpler and faster.

• Try cooking large amounts and then freezing in portions. This way, you'll always have a fast, prepared, low-effort meal at your fingertips.

• Preparing ingredients in advance will save time when you are ready to cook the meal later on. Peel and chop vegetables, for example, then keep them refrigerated in freezer bags until you need them.

a speedy food

Chicken appeals to cooks for many reasons, not least because it freezes exceptionally well (a chicken can be frozen with no effect on its flavor or texture for up to two years). However, its never-ending value as an ingredient in so many dishes can be found in the speed with which it can be cooked.

A whole bird, no matter how small, cannot be cooked in less than an hour, of course, but you should be able to cook the individual pieces of the chicken—a wing, a leg, a thigh, or a breast—within 30 minutes. When you are buying thighs, it can be worth paying a little extra to get them already deboned, so that you can flatten the meat or cut the flesh into chunks and thereby speed up the cooking process. If the recipe requires that you keep

the thighs whole, try to buy smaller thighs, because the larger they are, the longer they will take to cook. If small or boneless thighs are unavailable, you can speed up the cooking process by making a few fairly deep cuts into the surface of the meat. The same is true with chicken breast; flatten or score the meat and it will cook much quicker.

When preparing recipes that call for small pieces of chicken breast, many people use chicken tenders, thin chicken breast strips. These are easy to cook, so they may be worth the extra money. Chicken tenderloins from the edge of the breast closest to the bone may be cheaper but you'll have to remove the tendon.

and even stir-fried chicken can be low in fat, as long as you are careful about the amount of oil you put in the pan. The key to a successful low-fat diet is to mix up the flavors in your meals so that you don't get bored; expand your repertoire and try some new recipes.

Although chicken wings technically qualify as white meat as well, you should be aware that they are also the fattiest part of the bird. Be careful when you are barbecuing wings; they are prone to flare up because of the amount of fat that comes out when they cook. Chicken thighs and legs are still lean meat compared to other meats, such as beef and lamb. If you are watching your calorific intake, always make sure to remove the chicken skin; the majority of the fat is stored just under the skin.

great for family and friends

It seems that everybody likes chicken. When you are entertaining a large number of guests, you can almost guarantee that a chicken dish will be particularly well received. Similarly, when you are cooking for a roomful of youngsters, be they three or thirteen years old, chicken recipes will usually be devoured by even the fussiest of young diners. So defrost those chicken pieces you've got in the freezer, choose one of our delicious recipes, and dish up a beautiful feast for your family and friends in just minutes. No matter which recipe you choose from this book today, it is bound to be a sure-fire winner.

With the growth in demand for prepared foods, you can now find chicken in a host of different flavors. If you look in a delicatessen or the cooked meat aisle of a supermarket, you can find smoked chicken breast, which is wonderful in salads and on pizzas, cooked herbed chicken for sandwiches, and other interesting flavors, including Chinese chicken, barbecue chicken, and Cajun chicken.

a healthy choice

Another reason why chicken breast is such a popular choice these days is that it contains little fat. Steamed or broiled chicken breast is one of the leanest, healthiest meats available,

snacks & light bites

creamy chicken on bagels

Serves **4**
Total cooking time **30 minutes**

4 **bagels**, halved
2 tablespoons **prepared garlic butter**, softened
2 tablespoons **olive oil**
1 small **onion**, chopped
2 **boneless, skinless chicken breasts**, sliced
3 cups quartered **cremini mushrooms**
2 tablespoons **sherry**
1 cup **crème fraîche** or **cream cheese**
2 tablespoons chopped **flat leaf parsley**
salt and **black pepper**

Place the bagel halves, cut side up, on a baking sheet, spread the garlic butter over them and bake in a preheated oven, at 375°F, for 10–15 minutes, until crisp.

Meanwhile, heat the oil in a skillet, add the onion, and sauté for 3 minutes. Add the chicken and cook for 5 minutes. Add the mushrooms cook for another 5 minutes, until tender. Add the sherry and let simmer, then stir in the crème fraîche or cream cheese and parsley and season with salt and black pepper. Simmer, stirring, adding a little water if the mixture is too thick, until the chicken is cooked through. Spoon it over the baked bagels and serve.

For garlic baked mushrooms with chicken, put 4 large portobello mushrooms, stem side up, on a baking sheet. Dot with 2 tablespoons prepared garlic butter, season with salt and black pepper, and bake in a preheated oven, at 400°F, for 15 minutes, until tender. Meanwhile, cook 1 small onion and 2 chopped boneless, skinless chicken breasts in 1 tablespoon olive oil for 5 minutes. Stir in 1 cup crème fraîche or cream cheese and 2 tablespoons chopped flat leaf parsley. Season with salt and black pepper and simmer for 5 minutes, adding a little water if the mixture becomes too thick, until the chicken is cooked through. Spoon the baked garlicky mushrooms over the chicken to serve. **Total cooking time 20 minutes.**

cajun chicken & avocado melt

Serves **2**

Total cooking time **10 minutes**

1 small **ciabatta loaf**, halved
  lengthwise
2 tablespoons **tomato relish**
  or **salsa**
2 **tomatoes**, sliced
4 oz **cooked Cajun-spiced
  chicken breast**, sliced
1 small **avocado**, pitted,
  peeled, and sliced
4 oz **mozzarella cheese**,
  sliced

Put the ciabatta halves, cut side down, on an aluminum foil-lined broiler pan and toast under a preheated medium broiler for a few minutes, until crisp and hot. Turn over the bread and spread with the tomato relish or salsa. Arrange the tomato slices on top, followed by the chicken, avocado, and finally the mozzarella.

Place under the broiler and cook for 5 minutes or until the cheese has melted and the topping is hot.

For Cajun chicken hot open sandwich mix together 2 cups shredded cheddar or American cheese, 1 teaspoon Cajun seasoning mix, a pinch of cayenne pepper, ½ beaten egg, and 1 tablespoon beer. Toast 2 large slices of crusty bread on both sides, then top with 1 sliced cooked chicken breast and 2 sliced tomatoes. Spread the cheese mixture over the top and cook under the broiler until golden and bubbling. **Total cooking time 10 minutes.**

chicken & goat cheese panini

Serves **4**

Total cooking time **20 minutes**

¼ cup **prepared pesto**

1 tablespoon **olive oil**

4 **panini rolls** or **4 small parbaked baguettes**, halved

2 **cooked chicken breasts**, sliced

12–16 pieces **sun-dried tomatoes in oil**, drained

1 (6 oz) log **goat cheese**, sliced

handful of **basil leaves**

Mix together the pesto and oil and brush over the cut side of the bottom halves of the panini rolls or baguettes. Top with the sliced chicken, sun-dried tomatoes, goat cheese, and basil. Cover with the top half of the rolls or baguettes.

Cook in a sandwich toaster or panini grill for about 5 minutes, until the bread is crisp and the filling is hot. Alternatively, cook in a hot skillet or ridged grill pan, pressing the rolls down firmly. Turn and cook on the other side.

For chicken & goat cheese pizza, spread ¼ cup tomato pizza topping sauce over a large prepared pizza crust. Top with 2 sliced cooked chicken breasts, 1 (4 oz) package crumbled goat cheese and a handful of black ripe olives. Drizzle with 1 tablespoon pesto mixed with 1 tablespoon olive oil and bake in a preheated oven, at 400°F, for 15 minutes or until the crust is crisp and the topping is hot. **Total cooking time 20 minutes.**

chicken quesadillas

Serves **4**
Total cooking time **30 minutes**

8 **soft flour tortillas**
1 cup canned **refried beans**
2 cups chopped
  cooked chicken
1 **red chile,** seeded and finely
  chopped
4 **tomatoes,** finely chopped
handful of **fresh cilantro,**
  coarsely chopped
1½ cups shredded **sharp
  cheddar cheese**
3 tablespoons **olive oil**
**lettuce and corn kernel
  salad**, to serve

Spread 4 of the tortillas with the refried beans, then top with the cooked chicken, chopped chile, tomatoes, cilantro, and shredded cheese. Cover with the remaining tortillas, pressing them together firmly.

Heat 1 tablespoon of the olive oil in a large skillet, add 1 quesadilla, and cook for 3 minutes on each side, until the cheese has melted and the quesadilla is golden and crisp. Remove from the pan and keep warm. Repeat with the remaining quesadillas, adding a little more oil, if necessary.

Cut into wedges and serve warm with a crisp lettuce and corn kernel salad.

For spicy chicken nachos, spread ½ (10–11 oz) package tortilla chips in the bottom of a large ovenproof dish. Dot with 1 cup canned refried beans, 1 cup chopped cooked chicken, and ¼ cup spicy tomato salsa. Sprinkle with 1 cup shredded cheddar cheese and place under a preheated medium broiler until the cheese has melted. Sprinkle with chopped fresh cilantro and serve. **Total cooking time 10 minutes.**

chicken salsa wraps

Serves **4**

Total cooking time **10 minutes**

¾ cup **fresh tomato salsa**

4 **soft flour tortillas**

2 cups chopped **cooked barbecue chicken**

¼ small **red cabbage**, shredded

2 **carrots**, shredded

4 **scallions**, cut into fine strips

⅔ cup **sour cream**

green salad, to serve

Spoon the tomato salsa onto the tortillas and spread it evenly. Place one-quarter of the chicken in the center of each one with some of the cabbage, carrots, and scallions.

Top with sour cream and roll up. Cut in half and serve with a green salad.

For balsamic chicken wraps, thinly slice 3 boneless, skinless chicken breasts and coat in a mixture of 2 tablespoons balsamic vinegar, 2 tablespoons olive oil, and 1 crushed garlic clove. Season with salt and black pepper. Cook the chicken, in batches, on a hot ridged grill pan or in a skillet for 1–2 minutes on each side, until cooked through. Put onto warmed soft flour tortillas with ¾ cup tomato salsa, ¼ small shredded red cabbage, 2 shredded carrots, and 4 scallions, cut into strips. Top with sour cream, roll up, and serve. **Total cooking time 30 minutes.**

spicy chicken naans

Serves **2**

Total cooking time **30 minutes**

¼ cup **plain yogurt**

1 tablespoon **medium–hot Indian curry paste**

2 tablespoons **lemon juice**

2 **boneless, skinless chicken breasts**, each cut into 8 pieces

1 small **red onion**, thinly sliced

1 small **green bell pepper**, cored, seeded, and thinly sliced

¼ cup **tomato puree** or **sauce**

2 **naans** or other **flatbreads**

4 oz **mozzarella cheese**, sliced

Mix together the yogurt, curry paste, and lemon juice. Add the chicken pieces and stir to coat. Place the chicken on an aluminum foil-lined broiler pan with the onion and bell pepper slices and cook under a preheated hot broiler for 5–8 minutes, turning occasionally, until the chicken is cooked and beginning to char at the edges and the onion and bell pepper slices have softened slightly.

Spread the tomato puree or sauce over the naans or flatbreads, then top with the chicken, onion, bell pepper, and mozzarella. Line the broiler pan with a clean piece of foil. Place the naans or flatbreads on the foil, reduce the broiler to medium heat, and cook the naan "pizzas" for 5–8 minutes or until the cheese has melted and the topping is hot.

For spicy chicken & mango chutney chapati wraps,

mix 2 chopped boneless, skinless chicken breasts with ¼ cup plain yogurt, 1 tablespoon medium–hot Indian curry paste, and 2 tablespoons lemon juice. Transfer to an aluminum foil-lined broiler pan and cook under a preheated hot broiler for 5–8 minutes, turning occasionally, until cooked and beginning to char at the edges. Place on 2 warmed chapatis or tortillas with 1 thinly sliced small red onion, fresh cilantro leaves, and 2 tablespoons mango chutney. Roll up the chapatis and serve warm. **Total cooking time 20 minutes.**

chicken & ham sandwiches

Serves **4**

Total cooking time **10 minutes**

4 **ham** or **Canadian bacon slices**

8 **whole wheat bread slices**

2 teaspoons **whole-grain mustard**

4 crisp **iceberg lettuce leaves**

4 **tomatoes**, sliced

2 **cooked chicken breasts**, sliced

1 **avocado**, pitted, peeled, and sliced

Heat the ham or Canadian bacon slices in a dry skillet until warmed through.

Meanwhile, toast the whole wheat bread on both sides, then spread 4 slices with the whole-grain mustard.

Place a lettuce leaf on each of the toast with mustard and top with the sliced tomato. Divide the chicken among the 4 stacks.

Top with the ham or bacon and the avocado.

Finish with the remaining slices of toast and, using toothpicks to keep the sandwiches together, cut on the diagonal to serve.

For stuffed chicken breasts, make a slit down the sides of 4 boneless, skinless chicken breasts (about 5 oz each) to form pockets. Stuff each pocket with 6 oz sliced Fontina or Gruyère cheese and a handful of basil. Wrap each chicken breast with 2 slices of prosciutto. Place on a baking sheet and cook in a preheated oven, at 400°F, for 20 minutes or until cooked through. Meanwhile, heat 2 tablespoons olive oil in a skillet and toss in 1 (6 oz) baby spinach and 12 cherry tomatoes. Cook briefly until the spinach starts to wilt. Serve the chicken breasts on a bed of wilted spinach. **Total cooking time 30 minutes.**

chicken salad wraps

Serves **4**
Total cooking time **10 minutes**

4 **soft flour tortillas**
¼ cup **mayonnaise**
4 teaspoons **mango chutney**
2 **carrots**, shredded
2 **cooked chicken breasts**,
   shredded
¼ small **green cabbage**,
   thinly shredded
2 **tomatoes**, sliced
small handful of **fresh
   cilantro leaves**
salt and **black pepper**

Lay the tortillas on the work surface and spread each one with 1 tablespoon of the mayonnaise and 1 tablespoon of the mango chutney.

Divide the remaining ingredients among the tortillas and season with salt and black pepper. Roll up the wraps to serve.

For chicken club sandwich, broil 8 unsmoked bacon slices under a preheated hot broiler for 3–4 minutes on each side until crisp. Toast 12 slices of bread for 2–3 minutes on each side or to your preference. Spread 4 slices of the toast with 2 tablespoons mayonnaise. Top the slices with some shredded iceberg lettuce, 3 sliced tomatoes, and the bacon. Spread 4 more slices of toast with 2 tablespoons mango chutney and place on top of the bacon. Cover the mango with 2 sliced cooked chicken breasts and 1 thinly sliced small red onion. Top with the remaining slices of toast and secure each sandwich with 2 toothpicks. Slice in half diagonally to serve. **Total cooking time 20 minutes.**

chicken & apple soup in a mug

Serves **4–6**

Total cooking time **10 minutes**

2 tablespoons **vegetable oil**

1 **onion**, coarsely grated

1 **garlic clove**, crushed

3 tablespoons **medium–hot Indian curry paste**

½ teaspoon **ground turmeric**

4 cups hot **chicken broth**

1 small **apple**, peeled and grated

2 cups **cooked long-grain white rice**

2½ cups bite-size **cooked chicken** pieces

3 cups small **croutons**

chopped **fresh cilantro**, to garnish

Heat the oil in a large saucepan, add the onion and garlic, and sauté over medium-high heat for 3–4 minutes, stirring frequently, until softened.

Add the curry paste and turmeric, stir for 1 minute, then add the broth, apple, and rice. Simmer for 3–4 minutes to thicken slightly.

Stir in the chicken, then ladle the soup into large mugs. Top with the croutons and the cilantro.

For quick chicken & apple soup, heat 2 tablespoons vegetable oil in a large saucepan and add 1 chopped onion, 2 chopped garlic cloves, 1 chopped carrot, and 2 chopped potatoes. Cook over medium heat for 6–7 minutes, stirring frequently. Stir in 2 tablespoons medium Indian curry paste and cook for 1 minute. Add 5 cups hot chicken broth and 1 peeled and grated small apple. Bring to a boil and simmer for 8–10 minutes, until tender. Blend to the desired consistency, or leave chunky, then stir in 1 cup cooked long-grain white rice and 2 cups shredded cooked chicken. Ladle into bowls and serve garnished with croutons and fresh cilantro, if desired. **Total cooking time 20 minutes.**

ginger chicken soup

Serves **4**

Total cooking time **20 minutes**

1 tablespoon **peanut oil**

1 inch piece of **fresh ginger root**, peeled and grated

10 oz **boneless, skinless chicken breasts**, cut into strips

4 cups hot **chicken broth**

8 oz **dried egg noodles**

4 **bok choy**, sliced

2 tablespoons **sesame seeds**

Heat the oil in a wok or large saucepan, add the ginger, and stir-fry for 1 minute, then stir in the chicken and ½ cup of the broth. Bring to a boil, then cook over high heat for 5 minutes or until the chicken is cooked through.

Add the remaining broth and bring to a simmer. Stir in the noodles and cook according to package directions until the noodles are tender, adding the bok choy for the final 5 minutes of the cooking time.

Meanwhile, heat a nonstick skillet over medium-low heat and dry-fry the sesame seeds for 2 minutes, stirring frequently, until golden brown and toasted.

Ladle the soup into bowls and serve sprinkled with the toasted sesame seeds.

For ginger chicken wraps, heat 1 tablespoon olive oil in a skillet, add 1 lb thinly sliced boneless, skinless chicken breasts, 1 tablespoon peeled and grated fresh ginger root, 2 diced garlic cloves, and 6 sliced scallions, and cook, stirring, for 5–6 minutes or until the chicken is cooked through. Divide the chicken among 4 tortilla wraps, then top with 1 red and 1 yellow bell pepper, both cored, seeded, and sliced, and ½ shredded romaine lettuce. Roll up the wraps and serve. **Total cooking time 10 minutes.**

chicken caesar salad

Serves **4**
Total cooking time **10 minutes**

½ **ciabatta loaf**, cubed

2 tablespoons **olive oil**

1 **romaine lettuce**, leaves
  separated

1½ cups chopped
  cooked chicken

8 **cooked crispy bacon
  slices**, broken into pieces

⅓ cup **prepared Caesar
  salad dressing**

1 oz **Parmesan cheese
  shavings**

Place the ciabatta cubes on an aluminum foil-lined broiler pan and drizzle with the olive oil. Toast under a preheated medium broiler for about 5 minutes, turning occasionally, until golden and crisp.

Meanwhile, coarsely tear the lettuce leaves and put into a salad bowl with the chicken and most of the bacon pieces.

Add the toasted bread cubes and salad dressing and toss well to mix. Sprinkle with the reserved bacon pieces and the Parmesan shavings. Serve immediately.

For chicken Caesar with garlicky croutons, cut
½ ciabatta loaf into cubes. Mix 1 crushed garlic clove and ¼ cup olive oil and toss the cubes in the oil. Spread on a baking sheet and bake in a preheated oven, at 400°F, for 10 minutes, until crisp. Add to a bowl of torn romaine lettuce, chopped cooked chicken, and crispy bacon pieces tossed in ⅓ cup prepared Caesar salad dressing. **Total cooking time 20 minutes.**

hot & sour chicken salad

Serves **4**

Total cooking time **10 minutes**

2 cups coarsely chopped
cooked chicken

5 cups **salad greens**

2 cups thinly sliced **white
button mushrooms**

1 **red chile,** seeded and
finely chopped

1 small bunch of **fresh
cilantro,** leaves stripped
and chopped

1 tablespoon **Thai red
curry paste**

¼ cup **vegetable oil**

2 tablespoons **lime juice**

2 tablespoons coarsely
chopped **roasted salted
cashew nuts** (optional)

Toss the chicken in a large bowl with the salad greens,
mushrooms, chopped chile, and cilantro, then divide
among 4 plates.

Put the red curry paste, vegetable oil, and lime juice
into a jar with a tight-fitting lid, then shake until
thoroughly combined. Drizzle the dressing over the
salad, sprinkle with the cashew nuts, if using, and
serve immediately.

For hot & sour chicken soup, put 2 cups chicken
broth or water into a large saucepan with ⅓ cup Thai
red curry paste and bring to a boil. Add 8 oz sliced
boneless, skinless chicken breasts, then reduce the
heat and simmer for 7–8 minutes, until the chicken is
cooked through. Stir in 1 cup coconut milk and 2 cups
thinly sliced white button mushrooms and simmer for
another 1–2 minutes, until the mushrooms are just
tender. Ladle into deep bowls, then squeeze some lime
juice over the top and serve garnished with chopped
cilantro leaves and a finely chopped seeded red chile,
if desired. **Total cooking time 20 minutes.**

tandoori chicken wings with raita

Serves **4**
Total cooking time **30 minutes**

2 tablespoons **tandoori paste**
1 teaspoon **cumin seeds**
⅓ cup **plain yogurt**
2 teaspoons **lemon juice**
8–12 **chicken wings**
   (about 1 ½ lb)

Raita
½ **cucumber**
1 cup **plain yogurt**
2 teaspoons **lemon juice**
½ teaspoon **ground cumin**
salt and **black pepper**

To serve
½ **iceberg lettuce**, shredded
4–8 **poppadums, flatbreads**,
   or **crackers**

Mix the tandoori paste, cumin seeds, yogurt, and lemon juice in a large, shallow dish. Make 2–3 shallow cuts in each chicken wing and put into the dish. Use your fingers to coat the chicken wings thoroughly with the tandoori yogurt.

Arrange the wings in a single layer on an aluminum foil-lined baking sheet and cook in a preheated oven, at 425°F, for 20–25 minutes, until slightly charred and the juices run clear when the thickest part of the chicken is pierced with the tip of a sharp knife.

Meanwhile, make the raita. Halve the piece of cucumber lengthwise and use a spoon to remove the seeds. Shred the flesh and put into the middle of a clean dish towel, then bring up the edges and twist the cucumber in the dish towel over a sink to squeeze out the excess moisture. Put the cucumber into a bowl, add the yogurt, lemon juice, and ground cumin, then season and chill until the chicken is cooked.

Serve the cooked chicken wings with the shredded lettuce, chilled raita, and crisp poppadums, flatbreads, or crackers.

For tandoori chicken pita pockets, mix 1 tablespoon tandoori paste in a bowl with ⅔ cup plain yogurt, 1 tablespoon chopped mint, ½ teaspoon ground cumin, 2 teaspoons lemon juice, and plenty of salt and black pepper. Fold in 2 cups diced cooked chicken and stir thoroughly to coat, then spoon into 4 large, warmed whole wheat pita breads. Add some shredded lettuce and serve immediately. **Total cooking time 10 minutes.**

chicken & zucchini kebabs

Serves **4**

Total cooking time **20 minutes**

16 **unsmoked bacon slices**

2 **zucchini**, each cut into
   16 pieces

3 **boneless, skinless
   chicken breasts**, each
   cut into 8 pieces

1 tablespoon **sunflower oil**

2 tablespoons **honey**

1 tablespoon **whole-grain
   mustard**

To serve

corn kernels

peas

Soak 8 small wooden skewers in water. Stretch each bacon slice with the back of a knife. Cut each slice in half and wrap around a piece of zucchini. Thread onto 8 skewers, alternating the zucchini with pieces of chicken.

Put the kebabs onto an aluminum foil-lined broiler pan. Warm the oil, honey, and mustard together in a small saucepan, brush over the kebabs, and cook under a preheated medium broiler for 10 minutes, turning occasionally and brushing with any remaining honey mixture, until the bacon is crisp and the chicken is cooked through. Serve with corn kernels and peas.

For chicken, bacon & zucchini baguettes, cut 2 zucchini into slices lengthwise and put onto an aluminum foil-lined broiler pan. Brush the zucchini with a little oil, honey, and mustard and broil with 4 bacon slices for about 5 minutes, until the zucchini is tender and the bacon is crisp. Cut a baguette into 4 pieces and cut in half lengthwise. Butter and fill with 2 cups sliced cooked chicken and the zucchini and bacon. **Total cooking time 10 minutes.**

lemon, mint & chicken skewers

Serves **4**
Total cooking time **20 minutes**

⅔ cup **Greek yogurt**
finely grated zest and juice
  of 1 **lemon**
2 tablespoons chopped **mint**
2 tablespoons **olive oil**
4 **boneless, skinless
  chicken breasts**, each
  cut into 8 pieces
salt and **black pepper**

To serve
pita breads, warmed
sliced **cucumber**
sliced **radish**

Soak 8 small wooden skewers in water. Mix together the yogurt, lemon zest and juice, mint, and olive oil. Add the chicken pieces and stir well to coat.

Thread the chicken onto the skewers and put onto an aluminum foil-lined broiler pan. Cook under a preheated hot broiler for about 10 minutes, turning occasionally, or until the chicken is cooked and slightly charred at the edges. Slide the chicken off the skewers and serve in warm pita breads with slices of cucumber and radish.

For lemon chicken pita pockets, make a lemon mint dressing by mixing together 2 tablespoons mayonnaise, 2 tablespoons Greek yogurt, 1 teaspoon finely grated lemon zest and 1 tablespoon chopped mint. Warm 4 pita breads and fill with sliced cooked chicken, sliced cucumber, and sliced radish. Top with the lemon mint dressing. **Total cooking time 10 minutes.**

fennel, chicken & tomato pizza

Serves **2**

Total cooking time **30 minutes**

2 tablespoons **olive oil**
1 small **onion**, sliced
1 **garlic clove**, crushed
1 small head of **fennel**,
   thinly sliced
3 **tomatoes**, chopped
pinch of **sugar**
1 tablespoon **tomato paste**
1 (6½ oz) package
   pizza crust mix
1 cup chopped
   cooked chicken
8 **cherry tomatoes**, halved
4 oz **mozzarella cheese**,
   sliced
salt and **black pepper**

Heat the olive oil in a skillet, add the onion, garlic, and fennel, and cook for 3 minutes. Add the tomatoes, sugar, and tomato paste and simmer for 5 minutes, until the mixture is soft and pulpy. Season with salt and black pepper.

Meanwhile, make the pizza crust according to the package directions. Knead lightly until smooth, shape into a ball, and roll out thinly to a circle about 12 inches across. Place on a baking sheet.

Spread the tomato and fennel sauce over the pizza crust and sprinkle with the chicken and cherry tomatoes. Arrange the mozzarella on top and bake in a preheated oven, at 425°F, for 15 minutes, until crisp and golden.

For fennel, chicken & tomato pasta, heat 2 tablespoons olive oil in a saucepan, add 1 chopped onion, 1 crushed garlic clove, 2 cups chopped cooked chicken, and 1 chopped small head of fennel. Cook for 3 minutes, then add 3 chopped tomatoes and ⅔ cup tomato puree or sauce and simmer for 5 minutes. Season with salt and black pepper and stir in a handful of pitted black ripe olives. Serve with freshly cooked pasta. **Total cooking time 20 minutes.**

chicken & asparagus calzone

Serves **2**
Total cooking time **30 minutes**

12 **asparagus spears**,
  trimmed and cut into
  1 inch pieces
1 (6½ oz) package
  pizza crust mix
1 **cooked smoked
  chicken breast**, sliced
4 oz **Roquefort** or other
  blue cheese, crumbled
  (about 1 cup)
salt
arugula, to serve

Cook the asparagus in lightly salted boiling water for 3 minutes, until just tender, then drain.

Meanwhile, make the pizza crust mix according to the package directions. Knead lightly until smooth, then roll out thinly to make a large circle, about 12 inches across, then place on a baking sheet.

Sprinkle the chicken, asparagus, and crumbled blue cheese over half the dough, leaving a ½ inch border. Brush the edges with water, fold the dough over to cover the filling, and press the edges firmly to seal. Bake in a preheated oven, at 425°F, for 15 minutes, until crisp and golden. Serve warm with arugula.

For smoked chicken, asparagus & blue cheese salad

, cook 12 asparagus spears in lightly salted boiling water for 3 minutes, until just tender, then drain. Put 5 cups mixed salad greens into a bowl. Add the asparagus, 1 sliced, cooked smoked chicken breast, and a handful of pine nuts. Drizzle with a prepared blue cheese salad dressing and toss lightly to mix. **Total cooking time 10 minutes.**

chicken souvlaki

Serves **4**
Total cooking time **30 minutes**

3 tablespoons **olive oil**
3 tablespoons **red wine**
1 teaspoon **dried oregano**
finely grated zest and juice
    of 1 **lemon**
1 **garlic clove**, crushed
4 **boneless, skinless chicken
    breasts**, cut into strips
4 **pita breads**, warmed
    and split open
salt and **black pepper**

To serve
shredded **cabbage**
chopped **cucumber**
chopped **tomato**
chili sauce

Mix together the olive oil, wine, oregano, lemon zest and juice, and garlic in a large bowl. Season with salt and black pepper, add the chicken, mix well, and let marinate for 15 minutes.

Thread the chicken onto metal skewers and put onto an aluminum foil-lined broiler pan. Cook under a preheated hot broiler for 8–10 minutes, turning occasionally, until the chicken is cooked and beginning to char at the edges.

Slide the chicken off the skewers into the warm pita breads and add some shredded cabbage, chopped cucumber, chopped tomato, and a dash of chili sauce.

For hot chicken & hummus pita pockets, stir-fry 8 oz chicken strips in 1 tablespoon olive oil with ½ teaspoon dried oregano, 1 teaspoon garlic paste, and the grated zest of ½ lemon for 5 minutes, until cooked through. Warm 4 pita breads, cut in half widthwise, and open out to form pockets. Add the chicken with ¼ cup prepared hummus and romaine lettuce and serve. **Total cooking time 10 minutes.**

parmesan chicken cutlets

Serves **4**

Total cooking time **20 minutes**

2 **boneless, skinless chicken breasts**, halved horizontally

2 tablespoons **all-purpose flour**

1 **egg**, beaten

2 cups **fresh ciabatta bread crumbs**

1 cup freshly grated **Parmesan cheese**

3 tablespoons **sunflower oil**

4 small **baguettes**, cut in half lengthwise

¼ cup **mayonnaise**

4 small handfuls of **mixed salad greens**

salt and **black pepper**

Place the chicken halves between 2 pieces of plastic wrap and beat with a rolling pin to flatten slightly. Put the flour on a plate and the egg in a dish. On a separate plate, mix together the bread crumbs and Parmesan and season with salt and black pepper.

Coat each piece of chicken lightly in flour, shaking off any excess, dip into the beaten egg, and coat in the bread crumb mixture, pressing them on firmly.

Heat the oil in a large skillet, add the chicken, and cook for about 5 minutes on each side, until golden, crisp, and cooked through.

Fill the baguette pieces with mayonnaise, salad greens, and the hot chicken.

For chicken Caesar baguettes, stir-fry 2 boneless, skinless chicken breasts, cut into strips, in 2 tablespoons sunflower oil for about 5 minutes or until cooked through. Pile onto 4 pieces of French bread with mixed salad greens and a drizzle of prepared Caesar salad dressing. **Total cooking time 10 minutes.**

cheesy chicken omelet

Serves **2**

Total cooking time **10 minutes**

4 eggs

1 tablespoon **cold water**

1 tablespoon **butter**

½ cup chopped **cooked chicken**

½ cup shredded **Gruyère, Swiss**, or **American cheese**

salt and **black pepper**

salad, to serve

Put a small, nonstick skillet on the stove to heat. Crack the eggs into a bowl, season with salt and black pepper, and add the measured water. Beat with a fork until evenly mixed.

Add the butter to the pan. When it is foaming and melted, pour in the beaten egg mixture. As the eggs begin to set, use a wooden spoon to draw the mixture into the center of the pan, letting the runny egg flow to the edge of the pan.

Cook until the top of the omelet is softly set, then arrange the chicken and cheese down the center. Starting at the side nearest the handle, flip the omelet over the filling and then turn it out onto a plate. Cut in half and serve with a simple salad.

For chicken & cheese frittata, beat together 4 eggs and season with salt and black pepper. Heat 1 tablespoon olive oil in a small skillet with a heatproof handle. Add 2 chopped cooked russet or Yukon gold potatoes and cook for 5 minutes, until golden. Add 2 chopped scallions, ½ cup chopped cooked chicken, and a handful of frozen peas. Heat through, then pour the eggs over the vegetables. Cook until just set. Arrange 2 oz sliced Gruyère, Swiss, or American cheese on top and cook under a preheated broiler until the frittata is just firm and the cheese has melted. **Total cooking time 20 minutes.**

healthy feasts

chicken couscous salad

Serves **4**

Total cooking time **10 minutes**

1½ cups **couscous**

1 cup hot **chicken broth**

1 (15 oz) can **chickpeas (garbanzo beans)**, drained

1 cupdrained and chopped, **roasted peppers in oil from a jar**, with 3 tablespoons oil reserved

6 **cherry tomatoes**, halved

¼ cup chopped **mixed herbs**, such as parsley, mint, and fresh cilantro

1½ cups chopped **cooked barbecue chicken**

1 tablespoon **white wine vinegar**

1 teaspoon **Dijon mustard**

salt and **black pepper**

Put the couscous into a heatproof bowl, pour the hot broth over the grains, cover the bowl with plastic wrap, and let stand for 5–8 minutes, until the broth has been absorbed.

Meanwhile, in a large bowl, mix together the chickpeas (garbanzo beans), roasted peppers, tomatoes, herbs, and chicken.

Mix together the oil from the roasted peppers, the vinegar, and mustard in a small bowl. Season with salt and black pepper. Uncover the couscous, fluff up with a fork, add the dressing and chicken mixture, and stir well to mix.

For chicken & couscous stuffed bell peppers,

halve, core, and seed 4 red bell peppers, then roast in a preheated oven, at 425°F, for 20 minutes, until softened and lightly charred. Meanwhile, soak 1 cup couscous in ¾ cup hot chicken broth for 5–8 minutes or until the broth has been absorbed. Fluff up with a fork and stir in 6 halved cherry tomatoes, 3 tablespoons chopped mixed parsley, mint, and cilantro, 1 cup chopped cooked barbecue chicken, and (3 oz) chopped halloumi, mozzarella, or Muenster cheese. Spoon the mixture into the bell pepper halves, drizzle with a little olive oil, and cook under a preheated broiler for 5 minutes to brown. **Total cooking time 30 minutes.**

herb quinoa & chicken

Serves **4**
Total cooking time **30 minutes**

1 cup **quinoa**
1 tablespoon **olive oil**
1 **onion**, chopped
1 **garlic clove**, crushed
4 **boneless, skinless chicken breasts**, sliced
1 teaspoon **ground coriander**
½ teaspoon **ground cumin**
⅓ cup **dried cranberries**
½ cup chopped **dried apricots**
¼ cup chopped **parsley**
¼ cup chopped **mint**
finely grated zest of 1 **lemon**
salt and **black pepper**

Cook the quinoa in a saucepan of lightly salted boiling water for 15 minutes, until tender, then drain.

Meanwhile, heat the oil in a large skillet, add the onion, and sauté, stirring, for 5 minutes to soften. Add the garlic, chicken, cilantro, and cumin and cook for another 8–10 minutes, until the chicken is cooked.

Season the quinoa with salt and black pepper. Add the chicken mixture, cranberries, apricots, herbs, and lemon zest. Stir well and serve warm or cold.

For chicken & apricot Moroccan couscous, put ½ cup Moroccan-flavored couscous into a heatproof bowl, cover with boiling water, cover the bowl with plastic wrap, and let stand for 5–8 minutes. When all the water has been absorbed, stir in 2 cups chopped cooked chicken, 1 cup chopped dried apricots, and 1 cup rinsed and drained, canned chickpeas (garbanzo beans). **Total cooking time 10 minutes.**

yogurt chicken with greek salad

Serves **4**

Total cooking time **20 minutes**

⅔ cup **fat-free Greek yogurt**

1 **garlic clove**, crushed

2 tablespoons **olive oil**

finely grated zest and juice
   of 1 **lemon**

1 teaspoon **ground cumin**

4 **boneless, skinless
   chicken breasts**, cut
   into bite-size chunks

½ **cucumber**, chopped

1 **red onion**, sliced

4 **tomatoes**, cut into
   thin wedges

16 **pitted black ripe olives**

1 (6 oz) package **feta cheese**,
   crumbled (about 1 cup)

1 small **romaine lettuce**, torn

Dressing

1 tablespoon **lemon juice**

2 tablespoons **olive oil**

1 tablespoon chopped **fresh
   oregano** or ½ teaspoon
   dried oregano

Soak 8 small wooden skewers in water. In a bowl, mix together the yogurt, garlic, olive oil, lemon zest and juice, and cumin. Add the chicken and stir well. Thread onto the skewers and place on an aluminum foil-lined broiler pan.

Cook under a preheated hot broiler for 10 minutes, turning occasionally, or until the chicken is cooked and beginning to char in places.

Meanwhile, in a salad bowl, mix together the cucumber, onion, tomatoes, olives, feta, and lettuce.

Make the dressing by whisking together the lemon juice, oil, and fresh or dried oregano. Pour the dressing over the salad and lightly mix together. Serve with the chicken skewers.

For yogurt chicken & spinach ciabatta, prepare the chicken skewers as above. Slide the chicken off the skewers. Split a ciabatta loaf lengthwise and spread the bottom half with mayonnaise. Top with a handful of baby spinach, a few teaspoons of spicy tomato relish or salsa, and the hot chicken. Cover with the top half of the ciabatta loaf, then cut into 4 to serve. **Total cooking time 10 minutes.**

chicken pasta salad with pesto

Serves **4**
Total cooking time **20 minutes**

2 **boneless, skinless
  chicken breasts**
½ tablespoon **olive oil**
8 oz **conchiglie pasta**
¼ cup **walnut halves**
1 small **red onion**, sliced
1½ cups halved **baby
  plum tomatoes**
½ **cucumber**, cut into chunks
3½ cups **watercress** or other
  peppery salad greens
2 tablespoons **Parmesan
  cheese shavings**, to serve

Dressing
1½ tablespoons **olive oil**
2 tablespoons **prepared
  pesto**
1 tablespoon **balsamic
  vinegar**

Make the pesto dressing by whisking together all the ingredients in a small bowl and set aside.

Brush the chicken breasts with the oil, then cook in a preheated hot ridged grill pan for 12–15 minutes, turning once, until cooked through.

Meanwhile, cook the pasta in a saucepan of boiling water for 8–9 minutes, or according to the package directions, until "al dente." Drain, then refresh under cold running water and drain again.

Heat a nonstick skillet over medium-low heat and dry-fry the walnuts for 3–4 minutes, stirring frequently, until slightly golden.

Cut the chicken into thin slices, then place in a large bowl with the pasta, toasted walnuts, onion, tomatoes, cucumber, and watercress.

Toss with the pesto dressing and serve sprinkled with the Parmesan cheese shavings.

For chicken pesto baguettes, halve 4 baguettes horizontally and spread the bottoms of each with ½ tablespoon prepared pesto. Divide 2 cups peppery salad greens among the baguettes and top with 4 sliced tomatoes, ¼ sliced cucumber, ½ sliced red onion, and 2 sliced cooked chicken breasts. Top each with a dollop of mayonnaise, then replace the tops. **Total cooking time 10 minutes.**

curried chicken with avocado

Serves **4**

Total cooking time **10 minutes**

²/₃ cup **mayonnaise**

1 ½ teaspoons **mild curry powder**

1 teaspoon **ground allspice**

1 **red chile,** seeded and diced

juice of ½ **lime**

⅓ cup **mango chutney**

⅓ cup **Greek yogurt**

4 cups shredded **cooked chicken**

½ **iceberg lettuce,** leaves torn

1 cup **peppery salad greens**

2 **avocados,** pitted, peeled, and sliced

2 large **beefsteak tomatoes,** sliced

2 tablespoons **toasted slivered almonds**

Mix together the mayonnaise, curry powder, allspice, chile, lime juice, chutney, and yogurt in a large bowl, then stir in the chicken.

Place the lettuce on a serving plate, then top with the peppery salad greens, avocados, and tomatoes.

Spoon the chicken over the salad and serve sprinkled with the almonds.

For chicken kebabs with avocado dip, put 2 garlic cloves, 1 tablespoon grated fresh ginger root, and 3 chopped scallions in a mortar and pestle and grind to a paste. Stir in the juice of ½ lime, 1 tablespoon soy sauce, and 1 tablespoon vegetable oil. Put 4 ½ cups cubed boneless, skinless chicken breasts and 20 white button mushrooms into a bowl, pour the marinade over the top, and toss. Thread the chicken, mushrooms, and 20 cherry tomatoes onto 16 metal skewers. Cook in a preheated, hot ridged grill pan for 7–8 minutes on each side, until cooked through. Meanwhile, mix together 2 pitted, peeled, and mashed avocados, the juice of ½ lemon, 2 chopped tomatoes, and a pinch of dried red pepper flakes. Serve with the kebabs. **Total cooking time 30 minutes.**

chicken liver salad

Serves **4**
Total cooking time **10 minutes**

8 oz **bacon slices**
⅓ cup **olive oil**
7 slices **crusty bread**, cut into
    small cubes
1 lb **chicken livers**, halved
    and trimmed
3 cups **mixed peppery**
    salad greens
3 small **cooked fresh beets**,
    cut into wedges
1 **red onion**, sliced
1 tablespoon **raspberry**
    vinegar
1 tablespoon **Dijon mustard**
1 teaspoon **honey**

Cook the bacon under a preheated hot broiler or in a skillet for 6–8 minutes, until crisp.

Meanwhile, heat 1 tablespoon of the oil in a skillet, add the bread, and cook for 3–4 minutes, turning frequently, until golden. Remove from the pan with a slotted spoon and drain on paper towels.

Heat another tablespoon of the oil in the pan and cook the chicken livers for 2–3 minutes on each side, until golden brown but still slightly pink in the middle. Let cool slightly, then cut into bite-size pieces.

Toss together the mixed salad greens, beets, and onion in a serving bowl, then add the chicken livers and croutons. Top with the bacon.

Whisk together the remaining oil, vinegar, mustard, and honey in a small bowl and drizzle the dressing over the salad to serve.

For chicken liver & mustard pâté, melt 1 stick of butter in a skillet over medium heat, add 1 diced onion, and cook for 3–4 minutes. Add 1 crushed garlic clove and 1 lb trimmed and halved chicken livers and cook for 6–8 minutes, until cooked through. Stir in 1 tablespoon brandy and 1 teaspoon dry mustard and season well. Transfer to a food processor with 5 tablespoons melted butter and process until smooth. Pour into 4 small ramekins and let cool before serving. **Total cooking time 20 minutes.**

citrus chicken salad

Serves **2**

Total cooking time **10 minutes**

1 orange

4 cooked roasted chicken thighs

3 cups **watercress** or other **peppery salad greens**

1 **avocado**, pitted, peeled, and sliced

2 teaspoons **walnut** or **olive oil**

shelled walnut pieces (optional)

Place the orange on a cutting board and use a small, sharp knife to cut off the top and bottom so that you cut right through the peel and outside pith to the flesh. Now, cut the remaining peel and pith away from the flesh, cutting in strips downward, following the curve of the orange. Cut the orange into fleshy sections, using a sharp knife to carefully cut along each side of the inside pith. Discard the peel and pith, keeping only the sections.

Slice or shred the cooked chicken thighs, discarding the bones and skin, if preferred. Divide the watercress or peppery salad greens between 2 plates and arrange the orange sections, chicken, and sliced avocado attractively over the greens. Drizzle with walnut oil and sprinkle with a few walnut pieces, if desired.

For citrus baked chicken, wrap 4 rindless bacon slices around 2 boneless, skinless chicken breasts and pan-fry in 1 tablespoon olive oil over medium-high heat for 2 minutes on each side, until golden. Meanwhile, warm 1 cup orange juice in a saucepan with ½ teaspoon dried thyme and 2 teaspoons whole-grain mustard. Put the chicken into an ovenproof dish, pour the juice over the poultry, and bake in a preheated oven, at 400˚F, for about 20 minutes, until the chicken is cooked through. Slice thickly, arrange on 2 warm plates, drizzle with the orangey juices, and serve with a salad of peppery salad greens and avocado. **Total cooking time 30 minutes.**

chicken tacos

Serves **4**

Total cooking time **20 minutes**

1 tablespoon **vegetable oil**
1 lb **ground chicken**
2 **garlic cloves**, crushed
1 (1¼ oz) package **taco** or
   fajita seasoning mix
juice of **1 lime**
8 **taco shells**

To serve
tomato salsa
shredded **crisp lettuce**
Greek yogurt
lime wedges

Heat the oil in a skillet, add the ground chicken, and stir-fry, keeping the meat in clumps. Add the garlic and seasoning mix and continue cooking for 5 minutes, adding a little water if the mixture becomes too dry. Stir in the lime juice.

Warm the taco shells according to the package directions. Spoon in the chicken mixture and top with tomato salsa and shredded lettuce. Serve with lime wedges and yogurt on the side.

For Tex-Mex chicken & beans, cook 1 lb ground chicken in 1 tablespoon sunflower oil over high heat with 1 (1¼ oz) package taco or fajita seasoning mix for 5 minutes, until clumpy and cooked. Add 1 cup tomato puree or sauce and 1 cup rinsed and drained canned kidney beans. Heat through and serve on thick slices of toast from a crusty loaf. **Total cooking time 10 minutes.**

chicken dippers with hummus

Serves **4**

Total cooking time **10 minutes**

1 tablespoon **all-purpose flour**

1 tablespoon chopped **parsley**

1 tablespoon chopped **fresh cilantro**

12 oz **chicken strips**

2 tablespoons **butter**

1 tablespoon **olive oil**

Hummus

1 **garlic clove**, finely diced

1 (15 oz) can **chickpeas (garbanzo beans)**, rinsed and drained

juice of ½ **lemon**

2 tablespoons **tahini paste**

3–4 tablespoons **extra virgin olive oil**

Mix together the flour and herbs on a plate, then toss the chicken strips in the herbed flour.

Heat the butter and olive oil in a large skillet, add the chicken, and cook for 3–4 minutes on each side or until golden and cooked through.

Meanwhile, make the hummus. Put the garlic, chickpeas (garbanzo beans), lemon juice, and tahini into a food processor or blender and process until nearly smooth. With the motor still running, pour in the extra virgin olive oil through the feed tube and blend to the desired consistency.

Serve the chicken with hummus for dipping.

For spiced chicken breasts with hummus, mix together 1 crushed garlic clove and 1 ½ teaspoons each of paprika, dried thyme, cayenne pepper, and ground black pepper in a small bowl, then rub over 4 boneless, skinless chicken breasts (about 5 oz each). Cook the chicken breasts under a preheated hot broiler for 6–8 minutes on each side or until cooked through. Spoon 1 cup prepared hummus into a bowl. Serve the chicken with the hummus and an arugula salad. Total cooking time 20 minutes.

nectarine-glazed chicken kebabs

Serves **4**

Total cooking time **30 minutes**

2 **nectarines**, halved, pitted, and coarsely chopped

1 ½ inch piece of **fresh ginger root,** peeled and coarsely chopped

2 **garlic cloves**, chopped

1 teaspoon **soy sauce**

1 teaspoon **Worcestershire sauce**

2 teaspoons **olive oil**

1 ¼ lb **boneless, skinless chicken breasts**, cut into bite-size pieces

1 **red bell pepper**, cored, seeded, and cut into bite-size pieces

1 **yellow bell pepper**, cored, seeded, and cut into bite-size pieces

crisp green salad, to serve

Put the nectarines, ginger, garlic, soy sauce, Worcestershire sauce, and oil into a small food processor or blender and process until completely smooth.

Put the chicken and bell peppers into a nonreactive metal bowl and pour the marinade over them. Toss to mix, cover, and let marinate in the refrigerator for 5 minutes.

Thread the pieces of chicken and bell pepper onto metal skewers and cook under a preheated medium broiler or on a barbecue grill for 12–15 minutes, turning frequently, or until the chicken is cooked through.

Serve with a crisp green salad.

For chicken & nectarine salad, whisk together 1 tablespoon white wine vinegar, 3 tablespoons olive oil, 1 tablespoon chopped mint, 1 teaspoon honey, and ½ teaspoon Dijon mustard in a bowl. Toss together 3 halved, pitted, and sliced nectarines, 3 cups cubed, cooked chicken breasts, 1 chopped cucumber, ½ sliced red onion, and 2 cups arugula in a serving bowl. Toss with the dressing and serve with crusty bread. **Total cooking time 10 minutes.**

tandoori chicken skewers

Serves **4**
Total cooking time **30 minutes**

¾ cup **fat-free Greek yogurt**,
plus extra to serve
2 tablespoons **tandoori paste**
1 lb **boneless, skinless
chicken breasts**, cut
into strips
2 teaspoons **cumin seeds**
1 **small cucumber**
½ **red onion**, cut in half and
finely sliced
3 tablespoons **fresh cilantro
leaves**
2 **lemons**, cut into wedges
salt and **black pepper**
naans or other **flatbreads**,
warmed, to serve (optional)

Mix together the yogurt and tandoori paste in a large bowl, add the chicken, and toss until the chicken is well coated. Set aside to marinate for 10 minutes.

Heat a small, nonstick skillet over medium heat, add the cumin seeds, and dry-fry for 1–2 minutes, stirring frequently. Remove from the heat when the seeds become fragrant and begin to smoke.

Thread the chicken strips onto 8 small metal skewers and lay on an aluminum foil-lined baking sheet. Cook under a preheated hot broiler for 8–10 minutes, turning once, until the chicken is cooked through.

Meanwhile, slice the cucumber into ribbons, using a sharp vegetable peeler, and arrange on 4 serving plates. Sprinkle the onion and cilantro over the cucumber, sprinkle with the toasted cumin seeds, and season lightly with salt and black pepper. Place the chicken skewers and lemon wedges on top. Serve immediately with warm naans or other flatbreads and extra yogurt.

For tandoori chicken & salad naans, stir together 1 teaspoon tandoori paste and ⅓ cup fat-free plain yogurt in a bowl. Coarsely slice 2 cooked boneless, skinless chicken breasts and mix with the tandoori yogurt. Cut ½ cucumber into ribbons, using a vegetable peeler, and finely slice ½ red onion. Divide the chicken into 4 small naans, then divide the cucumber, onion, ½ teaspoon cumin seeds, and a few cilantro leaves among each naan. Squeeze a little lemon juice over the salad and serve immediately. **Total cooking time 10 minutes.**

chinese chicken wraps

Serves **4**

Total cooking time **10 minutes**

4 large **tortilla wraps**

¼ cup **plum sauce**, plus extra
to serve (optional)

2 **cooked boneless, skinless
sweet chili chicken breasts**,
sliced

½ **cucumber**, cut into batons

3 **scallions**, finely sliced
lengthwise

1 large **romaine lettuce heart**,
shredded

Spread the tortilla wraps with the plum sauce, then top each wrap with the chicken, cucumber, and scallions. Finish with the lettuce and roll up tightly.

Cut in half diagonally and serve with a little extra plum sauce, if desired.

For chicken phyllo pastries with plum sauce, mix together in a bowl 3 cups shredded, cooked chicken, 3 finely sliced scallions, 1 shredded carrot, 1 cup finely shredded snow peas, and 1 finely chopped small bunch of cilantro until combined. Cut 8 sheets of phyllo pastry to 6 x 10 inches. Put one-eighth of the chicken mixture along the end of one rectangle, leaving a gap at the edge. Fold in the longer pastry sides, then roll up into a log shape. Brush with melted butter to seal and repeat to make 8 pastries. Place on a lightly greased baking sheet and cook in a preheated oven, at 400°F, for 18–20 minutes, until golden and crisp. Serve with plum sauce. **Total cooking time 30 minutes.**

chicken with cilantro mayonnaise

Serves **4**

Total cooking time **20 minutes**

2 teaspoons coarsely crushed
   black peppercorns
4 **boneless, skinless chicken
   breasts**, thinly sliced
1 tablespoon **olive oil**

Cilantro mayonnaise

small bunch of **fresh cilantro**,
   leaves only
1 **garlic clove**, peeled
2 teaspoons **Dijon mustard**
1 **egg yolk**
2 teaspoons **white wine
   vinegar**
²/₃ cup **sunflower oil**
salt and **black pepper**

To serve
green salad
shredded **beets**

Make the cilantro mayonnaise. Reserve a few cilantro leaves for garnish and put the rest into a small food processor or blender with the garlic, mustard, egg yolk, and vinegar. Process until finely chopped. With the motor still running, slowly drizzle in the sunflower oil through the feed tube until the mixture is smooth and thick. Season with salt and black pepper.

Sprinkle the crushed peppercorns over the chicken slices and drizzle with the olive oil. Cook, in batches, on a preheated hot ridged grill pan for 1–2 minutes on each side or until cooked through and golden.

Serve the warm chicken slices with mixed salad greens, shredded beets, and the cilantro mayonnaise. Garnish with the reserved cilantro leaves.

For grilled chicken & tomato sandwiches, thinly
slice 3 boneless, skinless chicken breasts, season with salt and plenty of black pepper, and drizzle with 1 tablespoon olive oil. Cut 4 tomatoes in half, season, and drizzle with a little oil. Cook the chicken and tomatoes, in batches, on a preheated, hot ridged grill pan for 1–2 minutes on each side, until cooked and golden. Sandwich between slices of crusty multigrain bread with arugula and prepared garlic mayonnaise. **Total cooking time 10 minutes.**

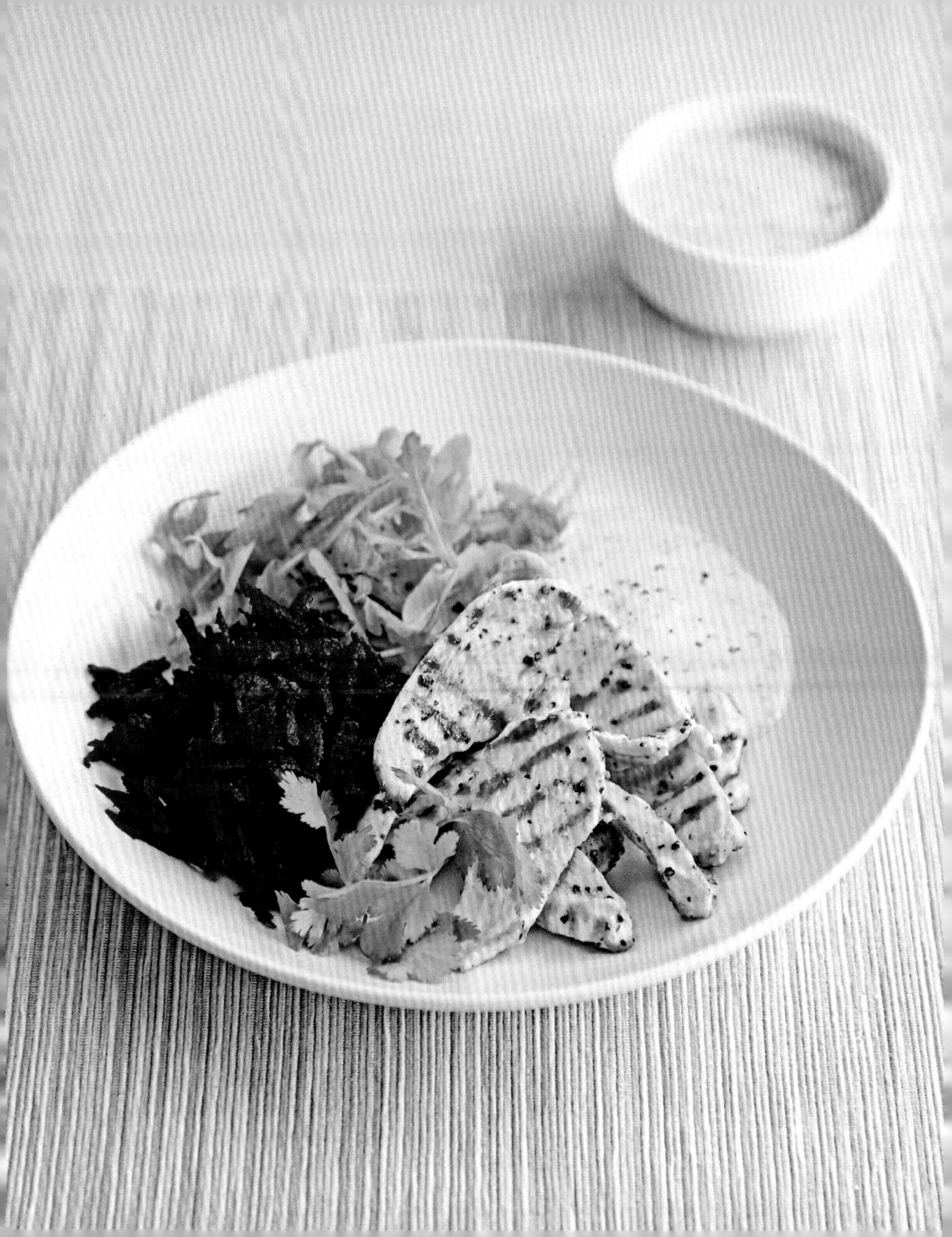

saucy lemon chicken with greens

Serves **4**

Total cooking time **30 minutes**

2 teaspoons **sesame oil**

4 **skinless, boneless chicken breasts**

1 **red chile,** seeded and chopped

finely grated zest of **1 lemon**

½ cup **lemon juice**

2 **bok choy,** halved

1 tablespoon **cornstarch,** mixed to a paste with 2 tablespoons water

Heat the sesame oil in a large, heavy skillet, add the chicken breasts, and cook for 5 minutes, turning once, or until browned. Add the chile to the pan with the lemon zest and juice. Cover and simmer for 15 minutes or until the chicken is cooked through.

Meanwhile, steam or lightly cook the bok choy in a little lightly salted boiling water until just tender.

Remove the chicken from the pan and keep warm. Stir the cornstarch paste into the pan juices and bring to a boil, stirring until thickened and adding a little water if the sauce is too thick. Serve the chicken with the bok choy and the lemon sauce poured over the top.

For lemon noodle chicken, stir-fry 8 oz chicken strips in 2 teaspoons sesame oil for 5 minutes or until browned and cooked through. Add ⅓ cup lemon stir-fry sauce, 1 (12 oz) package mixed stir-fry vegetables, and 1 (7 oz) package precooked stir-fry noodles. Cook, stirring, for 5 minutes, until the vegetables are tender, then serve. **Total cooking time 10 minutes.**

chicken & apricot stew

Serves **4**
Total cooking time **30 minutes**

1 tablespoon **olive oil**
2 **garlic cloves**, crushed
1 tablespoon peeled and
  grated **fresh ginger root**
1 large **onion**, chopped
1¼ lb **boneless, skinless
  chicken breasts**, cubed
½ cup **red split lentils**
1 teaspoon **ground cumin**
¼ teaspoon **ground
  cinnamon**
¼ teaspoon **ground turmeric**
¼ teaspoon **ground coriander**
12 **dried apricots**
juice of 1 **lemon**
3 cups hot **chicken broth**
1 tablespoon chopped **mint**
1 tablespoon chopped **fresh
  cilantro**
seeds of 1 **pomegranate**
2 tablespoons **toasted
  slivered almonds**
couscous, to serve

Heat the oil in a large saucepan, add the garlic, ginger, and onion, and cook for 1−2 minutes. Add the chicken and cook for another 5 minutes, stirring occasionally.

Add the lentils, spices, apricots, and lemon juice and stir well. Pour in the broth and bring to a boil, then reduce the heat and simmer for 15 minutes, until the chicken is cooked through.

Stir in the herbs and pomegranate seeds, then sprinkle with the almonds. Serve in bowls with couscous.

For chicken & apricot wraps, spread 4 tortilla wraps with 2 tablespoons mayonnaise. Top each with the leaves of ½ small butterhead lettuce, ½ cored, seeded, and sliced red bell pepper, 2 chopped dried apricots, a few cilantro leaves, ⅔ cup diced cooked chicken breasts, and 2 teaspoons mango chutney. Roll up the wraps and serve. **Total cooking time 10 minutes.**

honey-mustard chicken with slaw

Serves **4**
Total cooking time **20 minutes**

3 tablespoons **honey**
2 tablespoons **whole-grain mustard**
1 tablespoon **Worcestershire sauce**
1 tablespoon **dark soy sauce**
1 1/4 lb **chicken strips**
mixed leaf salad, to serve

Coleslaw
1/2 **red cabbage**, shredded
1/2 small **red onion**, thinly sliced
1 large **carrot**, shredded
1/4–1/3 cup **prepared Caesar dressing**

Put the honey, mustard, Worcestershire sauce, and soy sauce into a large bowl and mix to combine. Add the chicken strips and toss until the chicken is well coated in the glaze.

Scrape the chicken into an aluminum foil-lined roasting pan, spread out over the bottom, and then place in a preheated oven, at 400°F, for about 15 minutes, turning once, until cooked through.

Meanwhile, make the coleslaw. Combine the cabbage, red onion, and carrot in a large bowl, then mix with 1/4 cup of the Caesar dressing, adding more depending on the consistency desired.

Serve the glazed chicken on top of a mixed leaf salad together with the coleslaw.

For honey & mustard chicken slaw salad,

make a honey and mustard dressing by combining 1 tablespoon honey, 1 tablespoon whole-grain mustard, 1 1/2 tablespoons Worcestershire sauce, 2 teaspoons dark soy sauce, and 2–3 tablespoons freshly squeezed orange juice in a small bowl. In a large bowl, toss together 12 oz cooked chicken strips, 1/2 shredded red cabbage, 1/2 thinly sliced small red onion, and 1 shredded large carrot. Arrange the chicken and cabbage salad on serving plates, sprinkle with 4 cups prepared croutons and drizzle with the dressing. Serve immediately. **Total cooking time 10 minutes.**

chicken & eggplant casserole

Serves **4**
Total cooking time **30 minutes**

1 **eggplant**, thinly sliced
olive oil spray
6 **skinless chicken thighs**,
  chopped
1½ cups **prepared tomato
  and basil sauce**
4 oz **mozzarella cheese**,
  chopped
1 cup **fresh white bread
  crumbs**
2 tablespoons grated
  Parmesan cheese
salt and **black pepper**

Put the eggplant slices onto an aluminum foil-lined broiler pan and lightly spray with oil. Cook under a preheated broiler for about 5 minutes, turning once, or until tender.

Meanwhile, lightly spray a nonstick skillet with oil, add the chicken, and cook over high heat for 5 minutes or until cooked through. Stir in the tomato sauce and bring to a boil.

Put half the eggplant slices into the bottom of an ovenproof dish, pour the chicken and tomato mixture over the top, and cover with the remaining eggplant. Mix together the mozzarella, bread crumbs, Parmesan, and seasoning and sprinkle over the top. Bake in a preheated oven, at 400°F, for 15 minutes, until the topping is golden and crisp.

For chicken, eggplant & tomato soup, stir-fry 4 chopped boneless, skinless chicken thighs in 1 tablespoon olive oil with 1 chopped eggplant for 5 minutes or until cooked through. Stir in 2½ cups prepared tomato soup and heat through until hot. Serve with a swirl of low-fat yogurt. **Total cooking time 10 minutes.**

chicken with orange & olives

Serves **4**

Total cooking time **30 minutes**

2 tablespoons **olive oil**

4 **boneless, skinless chicken breasts** (about 5 oz each)

3 cups **chicken broth**

a few **thyme sprigs**

12 **black ripe olives**, pitted

2 **oranges**, divided into sections

1⅔ cups **bulgur wheat**

3 tablespoons **toasted slivered almonds**

2 tablespoons chopped **parsley**

salt and **black pepper**

Heat the oil in a large skillet, add the chicken, and cook for 3–4 minutes on each side, until browned. Pour in 2 cups of the broth, then stir in the thyme, olives, and orange sections. Cover and simmer for 15–16 minutes, until cooked through.

Meanwhile, put the bulgur wheat into a saucepan with the remaining broth, season, and simmer for 8–10 minutes, until most of the water is absorbed. Remove the pan from the heat and stir in the almonds, then cover and let stand.

Remove the chicken from the skillet and keep warm. Simmer the sauce for 4–5 minutes, until reduced by half. Stir in the chopped parsley.

Serve the chicken with the bulgur wheat, drizzled with the thyme, olive, and orange sauce.

For chicken, orange & olive sandwiches, toast 8 slices of whole wheat bread under a preheated hot broiler for 2–3 minutes on each side. Spread 4 of the slices with 2 teaspoons prepared pesto each, then top each with a small handful of mixed baby salad greens, a few orange sections, 2–3 slices of cooked chicken, 1 sliced tomato, and 2–3 sliced pitted olives. Top with the remaining toast and serve. **Total cooking time 10 minutes.**

sweet chili chicken stir-fry

Serves **4**

Total cooking time **25 minutes**

1 tablespoon **peanut oil**

1 lb **boneless, skinless chicken breasts**, cut into bite-size pieces

1 large **onion**, cut into large pieces

2 **garlic cloves**, sliced

1 tablespoon peeled and finely chopped **fresh ginger root**

⅔ cup **pineapple** chunks

1 cup **sweet chili stir-fry sauce**

1 cup halved **water chestnuts**

1 tablespoon **soy sauce**

1 tablespoon **lime juice**

1 cup **frozen peas**

2 tablespoons coarsely chopped **unsalted cashew nuts**

steamed **rice**, to serve

Heat the oil in a wok or large skillet over medium heat. Add the chicken pieces and cook for 3–4 minutes, stirring frequently, until golden brown all over. Remove from the heat with a slotted spoon and set aside.

Add the onion to the wok and stir-fry for 2–3 minutes, until golden and beginning to soften, then add the garlic and ginger and stir-fry for 1–2 minutes. Stir in the pineapple and sweet chili sauce, then bring to a boil.

Return the chicken to the pan with the water chestnuts, soy sauce, and lime juice and stir to combine. Reduce the heat and simmer gently for 4–6 minutes, until the chicken is cooked through, then add the peas and stir for 1–2 minutes, until hot. Sprinkle with the cashew nuts and serve immediately with steamed rice.

For quick sweet chili chicken stir-fry, heat 2 teaspoons peanut oil in a large skillet. Add 1 teaspoon each of finely chopped garlic and fresh ginger root. Stir-fry for 30 seconds. Add 1 (12 oz) package prepared stir-fry vegetables and cook for 3–4 minutes, then add 3 cups cooked chicken slices, ⅔ cup pineapple chunks, 1 cup sweet chili stir-fry sauce, 1 tablespoon soy sauce, and 1 tablespoon lime juice. Stir until hot, then spoon the mixture over 2½ cups hot cooked rice divided among 4 deep bowls. **Total cooking time 10 minutes.**

mild & creamy chicken curry

Serves **4**

Total cooking time **30 minutes**

1½ tablespoons **peanut oil**

1 large **onion**, sliced

2 **garlic cloves**, finely chopped

1 teaspoon **ground turmeric**

1 teaspoon **ground cumin**

1 teaspoon **ground coriander**

½ cup **korma paste**

1 lb **boneless, skinless
chicken breasts**, cubed

1 **large sweet potato** (about
8 oz), peeled and cubed

1 cup **coconut milk**

½ cup **water**

2 tablespoons **ground
almonds**

1⅓ cups **basmati** or other
long-grain rice, rinsed

salt and **black pepper**

fresh cilantro, to garnish

naans or other **flatbreads**,
warmed, to serve

Heat the oil in a saucepan or deep skillet over medium heat, add the onion, and cook for 5–6 minutes, stirring frequently, until softened.

Add the garlic, spices, and korma paste and stir-fry for 1–2 minutes, then stir in the chicken and sweet potato. Cook for 3–4 minutes to seal the chicken, then add the coconut milk, water, and ground almonds and season with salt and black pepper. Bring to a boil, then reduce the heat and simmer gently for 12–15 minutes, until the chicken is cooked through and the potato is tender.

Meanwhile, put the basmati or other long-grain rice into a large saucepan of lightly salted boiling water and cook for 12 minutes, or according to the package directions, until tender.

Serve the curry on a bed of rice, garnished with the cilantro and with naans or other flatbreads on the side, if desired.

For broiled korma chicken with rice, cut 3–4 deep slashes in 4 boneless, skinless chicken breasts (about 5 oz each), then cover each breast with 1 tablespoon korma paste. Put the chicken onto an aluminum foil-lined baking sheet and cook under a preheated hot broiler for 12–15 minutes, turning once, until cooked. Serve with 2½ cups cooked basmati rice, topped with a couple of dollops plain yogurt and with lemon wedges on the side. **Total cooking time 20 minutes.**

chicken pilaf with cauliflower

Serves **4**
Total cooking time **30 minutes**

1 tablespoon **sunflower oil**
1 **onion**, chopped
6 **boneless, skinless chicken
  thighs**, chopped
2 tablespoons **korma curry
  paste**
1 cup **basmati** or other
  long-grain rice
4 cups **chicken broth**
1 small **cauliflower**,
  cut into florets
1 cup trimmed **green bean
  halves** (cut widthwise)
2 **carrots**, shredded
¼ cup **toasted slivered
  almonds**
salt and **black pepper**
low-fat plain yogurt, to serve

Heat the oil in a large saucepan, add the onion and chicken, and cook, stirring, for 5 minutes. Stir in the curry paste, rice, broth, cauliflower, and green beans. Bring to a boil, reduce the heat, cover, and simmer for 10 minutes, until the broth has been absorbed, the rice and vegetables are tender, and the chicken is cooked through.

Stir in the shredded carrot, heat through for 1 minute, and season with salt and black pepper. Sprinkle with slivered almonds and serve with plain yogurt.

For curried chicken with vegetable rice, heat 2 tablespoons korma paste in a saucepan, add 1 ½ cups chopped cooked chicken, ½ (16 oz) package frozen mixed vegetables, and about ¼ cup boiling water. Cover and cook for 5 minutes, then stir in 2½ cups cooked long-grain rice and heat through, stirring, for 3 minutes, until hot. **Total cooking time 10 minutes.**

chicken & vegetable stir-fry

Serves **4**

Total cooking time **10 minutes**

2 tablespoons **coconut oil**

1¼ inch piece of **fresh ginger
root**, peeled and finely diced

2 **garlic cloves**, crushed

1 **onion**, chopped

1 lb **boneless, skinless
chicken breasts**, cut
into strips

2 cups quartered **white
button mushrooms**

4 cups **broccoli florets**

2 cups chopped **curly kale**

1–2 tablespoons **soy sauce**

2 tablespoons **sesame seeds**

Heat the oil in a wok or large skillet until hot, add the
ginger, garlic, and onion, and stir-fry for 30 seconds.
Add the chicken and stir-fry for another 2–3 minutes.

Add the vegetables, then sprinkle with the soy sauce.
Stir-fry for 1–2 minutes, then cover and steam for
another 4–5 minutes, until the vegetables are tender
and the chicken is cooked through.

Serve sprinkled with the sesame seeds.

For chicken & Asian vegetable stir-fry, heat
2 tablespoons coconut oil in a wok until hot, add
6 chopped scallions, 2 crushed garlic cloves, and
1 tablespoon peeled and grated fresh ginger root,
and stir-fry for 2 minutes. Add 1 lb sliced boneless,
skinless chicken breasts, and stir-fry for 2–3 minutes.
Add 6 baby corn and 1 cored, seeded, and sliced red
bell pepper and stir-fry for another 3–4 minutes. Stir in
4 oz chopped shiitake mushrooms, ½ cup bean sprouts,
and 2 chopped bok choy and stir-fry for 4–5 minutes.
Stir in 2 tablespoons oyster sauce and 1 teaspoon
soy sauce and cook for another 4–5 minutes. Serve
sprinkled with 2 tablespoons toasted sesame seeds.
Total cooking time 20 minutes.

moroccan fruity chicken stew

Serves **4**

Total cooking time **30 minutes**

1 tablespoon **olive oil**

1 large **red onion**, cut into
large chunks

1 **onion**, cut into large chunks

12 oz **boneless, skinless
chicken breasts**, diced

1 teaspoon **ground cumin**

1 teaspoon **paprika**

1 teaspoon **ground coriander**

½ teaspoon **ground
cinnamon**

½ teaspoon **ground ginger**

1 cup **dried prunes**

1 cup **dried apricots**

1 (15 oz) can **chickpeas
(garbanzo beans)**

2½ cups **rich chicken broth**

1 tablespoon **cornstarch**,
mixed to a paste with
2 tablespoons water

¼ cup chopped **fresh cilantro**

Heat the oil in a large, heavy saucepan, add the onions and chicken, and cook over medium-high heat for 10 minutes, stirring occasionally, or until golden in places and soft. Add the spices, stir, and cook for another 2 minutes to help the flavors develop.

Stir in the prunes and apricots, chickpeas (garbanzo beans), and broth and bring to a boil. Cover and cook for 15 minutes, until all the ingredients are soft and cooked through.

Add the cornstarch paste and stir well to thicken slightly, then stir in the fresh cilantro. Serve with couscous, if desired.

For Moroccan chicken & bean soup, heat

1 tablespoon olive oil in a saucepan, add 1 thinly sliced red onion and 2 cups thinly sliced chicken breasts, and cook for 3–4 minutes. Add 1 teaspoon ground cumin, 1 teaspoon ground coriander, and ½ teaspoon ground cinnamon and cook for 30 seconds. Pour in 2½ cups chicken broth and 1 drained (15 oz) can chickpeas (garbanzo beans). Bring to a boil, then reduce the heat and add ½ cup coarsely chopped dried prunes. Cook for another 4 minutes, until piping hot and the chicken is cooked through. Process in a blender for a smooth soup, if desired. **Total cooking time 10 minutes.**

chicken & shrimp spring rolls

Serves **4**

Total cooking time **30 minutes**

½ (12 oz) package **mixed
  stir-fry vegetables**
1 tablespoon **sesame oil**
1 **red chile,** seeded and
  chopped
½ inch piece of **fresh ginger
  root**, peeled and grated
1½ cups chopped **cooked
  chicken**
4 oz **peeled small shrimp,**
  thawed if frozen, chopped
2 tablespoons **Chinese
  stir-fry sauce**, any flavor
6 sheets **phyllo pastry**
2 tablespoons **sunflower oil**
salt and **black pepper**
teriyaki sauce, for dipping

Chop the stir-fry vegetables to make the pieces slightly smaller, then put into a bowl. Add the sesame oil, chile, ginger, chicken, shrimp, and sauce. Season with salt and black pepper and mix well.

Work with 1 sheet of phyllo pastry at a time and keep the rest covered with plastic wrap to prevent them from drying out. Cut each sheet in half widthwise and put one-twelfth of the chicken mixture at one end of each strip. Roll it up, tucking in the ends as you roll. Put onto a baking sheet and brush with a little sunflower oil. Repeat with remaining sheets of phyllo and filling to make 12 rolls.

Bake in a preheated oven, at 400°F, for 15 minutes, until golden and crisp. Serve warm with teriyaki sauce for dipping.

For teriyaki chicken rolls, warm 12 thin pancakes (the kind used for crispy duck, available from Asian supermarkets) in the microwave according to the package directions. Fill with 2 cups cooked chicken, cut into strips, 6 scallions, cut into fine strips, and ¼ cucumber, cut into sticks. Top with a little teriyaki sauce, roll up, and serve. **Total cooking time 10 minutes.**

chicken & mozzarella packages

Serves **4**
Total cooking time **30 minutes**

4 **skinless, boneless chicken
breasts** (about 5 oz each)
4 teaspoons **prepared red
chile pesto** or **mild harissa**
2 **plum tomatoes**, sliced
4 oz **mozzarella cheese**, cut
into 8 slices
1 small bunch of **basil**, leaves
stripped
8 thin slices of **chorizo**

To serve
4 cups **prepared healthy
couscous** or **bulgur
wheat salad**
arugula

Place the chicken breasts between 2 large sheets of
plastic wrap on a cutting board and beat with a rolling
pin to flatten; they need to be about ¼ inch thick.
Spread 1 teaspoon of the pesto or mild harissa evenly
over each flattened chicken breast.

Cover half of each chicken breast with 2–3 slices
of tomato and 2 slices of mozzarella, then fold the
uncovered half of the chicken over the filling to create
a sandwich. Sprinkle the basil leaves over the top of the
chicken packages, reserving a few to garnish.

Cover each package with 2 thin slices of the chorizo,
then secure with a wooden toothpick by threading it
through the chicken. Put the packages onto a large,
nonstick baking sheet, then cook in a preheated oven,
at 425°F, for 15–18 minutes or until cooked through.

Serve the chicken packages with the couscous or
bulgur wheat salad and arugula, garnished with the
reserved basil leaves.

For chicken & tomato salad with pesto dressing

arrange 3 cups sliced, cooked chicken breast on
serving plates with 5 cups arugula leaves and 12 cherry
tomatoes, halved. Top with 2 tablespoons Parmesan
cheese shavings. Whisk 2 tablespoons pesto into
3 tablespoons aged balsamic vinegar and drizzle the
dressing over the salad. Serve with warmed, sliced
flatbreads. **Total cooking time 10 minutes.**

crispy stuffed chicken breasts

Serves **4**

Total cooking time **30 minutes**

4 **skinless, boneless chicken breasts** (about 5 oz each)

½ cup **cream cheese**

1 large **garlic clove**, finely chopped

2 tablespoons chopped **parsley**

½ tablespoon **lemon juice**

1 teaspoon finely grated **lemon zest**

⅔ cup **all-purpose flour**

1 **extra-large egg**, beaten

¾ cup **dried white bread crumbs**

salt and **black pepper**

To serve
new potatoes
broccoli florets

Cut deep slits along the sides of the chicken breasts to create a pocket in each. Mix together the cream cheese garlic, parsley, and lemon juice and zest. Season well with salt and black pepper, then spoon the filling into the chicken.

Put the flour, egg, and bread crumbs into separate shallow dishes. Coat each chicken breast first in the flour, followed by the egg, and then the bread crumbs, and put onto a baking sheet. Cook the chicken in a preheated oven, at 425°F, for 15–18 minutes, until cooked through.

Serve the crisp baked chicken with steamed broccoli and boiled new potatoes.

For chicken breasts in garlic & herb bread crumbs,
mix together ¾ cup dried white bread crumbs with 1 teaspoon each of garlic powder and dried herbes de Provence in a shallow dish. Put ⅔ cup all-purpose flour into a separate dish and 1 beaten egg in another dish. Coat 1 lb chicken strips first in the flour, followed by the egg, and then the bread crumbs, and put onto a baking sheet. Place in a preheated oven, at 425°F, for 12–15 minutes, until cooked through, then serve with mashed potatoes and a mixed leaf salad. **Total cooking time 20 minutes.**

chicken koftas

Serves **4**

Total cooking time **20 minutes**

1 lb **ground chicken**
2 **garlic cloves**, crushed
1 teaspoon **ground cumin**
2 teaspoons **ground coriander**
2 teaspoons chopped **fresh cilantro**
1 cup **Greek yogurt**
1 tablespoon **mint sauce**
¼ **cucumber**, shredded and squeezed to remove excess liquid
salt and **black pepper**

To serve
4 **pita breads**, wamed and halved
salad greens
baby plum tomatoes, halved

Put the ground chicken, garlic, cumin, ground coriander, and fresh cilantro into a bowl. Season with salt and black pepper and mix well.

Using wet hands, make 12 even cylinder shapes from the mixture and thread onto metal skewers, pressing firmly. Cook under a preheated hot broiler for 10 minutes, turning occasionally, until cooked through and browned.

Meanwhile, mix together the yogurt, mint sauce, and cucumber. Take the koftas off the skewers and serve in warm pita breads with salad greens, tomatoes, and the yogurt dressing.

For quick chicken moussaka, cook 1 lb ground chicken in 1 tablespoon sunflower oil until browned. Add 1 crushed garlic clove, 1 teaspoon ground cumin, 2 teaspoons ground coriander, and 1 (14½ oz) can diced tomatoes. Simmer for 10 minutes. Meanwhile, thinly slice 1 eggplant, brush with a little oil, and cook in a hot skillet for 2 minutes on each side. Add the chicken mixture to a baking dish and arrange the eggplant slices on top. Cover with 1 cup Greek yogurt mixed with 1 egg. Cook under a preheated medium broiler until golden and bubbling. Serve with a green salad. **Total cooking time 30 minutes.**

hot &
spicy

chicken noodle broth

Serves **4**

Total cooking time **30 minutes**

4 **boneless, skinless chicken thighs** (about 12 oz)

5 cups **chicken** or **vegetable broth**

2 tablespoons **vegetable oil**

1 **red bell pepper**, cored, seeded, and sliced

4 **scallions**, cut into ¾ inch lengths

1 tablespoon peeled and chopped **fresh ginger root**

3 cups sliced **white button mushrooms**

8 oz **dried medium egg noodles**

1–2 tablespoons **dark soy sauce**

2 tablespoons chopped **fresh cilantro**

Put the chicken thighs into a saucepan and pour the broth over them. Bring to a boil, then reduce the heat and simmer gently for about 20 minutes or until the chicken is cooked through.

Meanwhile, heat the oil in a large saucepan or wok, add the red bell pepper and scallions, and cook for 4–5 minutes. Add the ginger and mushrooms and cook gently for another 4–5 minutes, until softened and golden.

Use a slotted spoon to remove the chicken thighs from the broth and set aside to cool slightly. Add the noodles to the broth, turn off the heat, cover, and set aside for 4–5 minutes, until just tender. Add the cooked vegetables and season with the soy sauce.

Once the chicken thighs are cool enough to handle, remove and discard the bones, then shred the meat and return to the soup. Ladle the soup and noodles into 4 large bowls. Sprinkle with the chopped cilantro and serve immediately.

For chicken noodle salad, cook 8 oz medium dried egg noodles according to the package directions. Cool under cold running water. Meanwhile, slice 1 red bell pepper, 4 scallions, and 8 oz white button mushrooms. Combine ¼ cup vegetable oil, 2 teaspoons sesame oil, if using, 2 tablespoons light soy sauce, and 2 teaspoons minced ginger (from a jar). Toss the cooled noodles with 3 cups shredded, cooked chicken breasts, the vegetables, and dressing, then serve immediately, sprinkled with 2 tablespoons chopped fresh cilantro, if desired. **Total cooking time 10 minutes.**

spicy chicken & rosemary soup

Serves **4**
Total cooking time **10 minutes**

2 (14½ oz) cans **cream of
  chicken soup**
2 **garlic cloves**, crushed
1 **red chile,** seeded and
  finely chopped, plus extra
  to garnish
2 tablespoons finely chopped
  rosemary
crusty bread rolls, to serve

To garnish
finely chopped **chives**
chili oil

Pour the soup into a saucepan, stir in the garlic, chile, and rosemary, and bring to a boil. Reduce the heat to medium and cook for a few minutes or until piping hot.

Remove from the heat. Ladle into bowls, sprinkle with the chives and the remaining chopped chile, to garnish, and drizzle with chili oil. Serve immediately with crusty bread rolls.

For spicy chicken & rosemary creamy pasta, cook 1 lb penne in a large saucepan of salted boiling water according to the package directions until "al dente." Meanwhile, heat 2 tablespoons olive oil in a large skillet, add 2 chopped garlic cloves, 2 seeded and finely chopped red chiles, and 1 lb chopped boneless, skinless chicken thighs, and cook over medium heat, stirring occasionally, for 8–10 minutes or until the chicken is sealed and cooked through. Add 1 teaspoon dried rosemary and 1 cup crème fraîche or heavy cream. Drain the pasta, add to the skillet, and season. Toss to mix well, then serve immediately with an arugula salad. **Total cooking time 20 minutes.**

curried chicken & grape salad

4 large **cooked chicken
breasts,** skin-on, cut into
bite-size pieces
large handful of **butterhead
lettuce**
12 **cherry tomatoes,** halved
1 1/3 cups **seedless green
grapes,** halved
6 **scallions,** thinly sliced

Curry mayonnaise
1 cup **mayonnaise**
2 teaspoons **medium** or
hot curry powder
finely grated zest and juice
of 1 **lemon**
1/2 cup finely chopped
fresh cilantro

Make the curry mayonnaise. Put all the ingredients
into a bowl and stir to mix well. Set aside.

Put the chicken, lettuce, tomatoes, grapes, and scallions
into a large salad bowl and mix well.

Spoon the mayonnaise over the salad, toss to mix well,
and serve with crusty bread, if desired.

For broiled chicken with curry mayonnaise,

make the curry mayonnaise as above. Put 4 boneless,
skinless chicken breasts (about 5 oz each), into a bowl.
Mix 1/3 cup olive oil, 1 teaspoon dried red pepper flakes,
2 teaspoons paprika, 2 crushed garlic cloves, and the
grated zest and juice of 1 lemon in a bowl, then season.
Pour the mixture over the chicken and toss. Cook
under a preheated hot broiler for 6–8 minutes on
each side or until cooked through. Cover and let rest
for 2–3 minutes. Serve with the curry mayonnaise
and salad. **Total cooking time 30 minutes.**

chicken & apricot couscous

Serves **4**
Total cooking time **20 minutes**

1 cup **couscous**
1 tablespoon **hot curry powder**
⅓ cup **extra virgin olive oil**
3 cups hot **chicken broth**
1 cup **cashew nuts**
finely grated zest and juice of 1 **lemon**
1 **red chile,** seeded and chopped
¼ cup chopped **mint**
¼ cup chopped **fresh cilantro**
¾ cup finely chopped **dried apricots**
⅔ cup **dried cranberries**
2 **cooked chicken breasts,** skin removed and coarsely shredded
juice of 1 **orange**
salt and **black pepper**
chopped **flat leaf parsley,** to serve

Put the couscous, curry powder, and oil into a large heatproof bowl. Stir in the broth, then cover with plastic wrap and let stand for 5–8 minutes, or according to the package directions, until the broth is absorbed.

Meanwhile, heat a small, nonstick skillet until hot, add the cashew nuts, and dry-fry, stirring frequently, for 3–4 minutes or until toasted. Remove from the pan and set aside.

Fork through the couscous to separate the grains, then stir in the cashews and all the remaining ingredients. Season, toss to mix well, and serve sprinkled with chopped parsley.

For spicy chicken & fruit couscous salad, put 3 cups shredded, cooked chicken breasts and 3 cups prepared heat & serve vegetable couscous into a large bowl. Mix together ¼ cup olive oil, 1 seeded and finely diced red chile, ⅓ cup chopped dried apricots, ⅓ cup dried cranberries, 1 teaspoon hot curry powder, and the juice of 2 limes in a bowl and season. Pour the dressing over the salad, toss, and serve. **Total cooking time 10 minutes.**

green chicken skewers

Serves **4**
Total cooking time **30 minutes**

1 ¼ lb **boneless, skinless chicken thighs**, cut into bite-size pieces

⅔ cup chopped **fresh cilantro**

⅔ cup chopped **mint**

1 teaspoon **coarse black pepper**

juice of 2 **lemons**

1 teaspoon packed **light brown sugar**

2 teaspoons peeled and finely grated **fresh ginger root**

2 **garlic cloves**, crushed

1 cup **plain yogurt**

lemon wedges, to serve

Dip

½ cup **rice** or **wine vinegar**

2 tablespoons **sugar**

1 **red chile,** finely diced

½ **red onion**, finely diced

⅓ cup finely diced **cucumber**

Put the chicken into a shallow, nonreactive bowl. Put the herbs, black pepper, lemon juice, sugar, ginger, garlic, and yogurt into a food processor or blender and blend until smooth. Pour the mixture over the chicken and toss to coat evenly, then cover and let marinate for 10–15 minutes.

Meanwhile, make the dip. Heat the vinegar and sugar in a small saucepan until the sugar has dissolved, then increase the heat and boil for 3 minutes, until slightly syrupy. Remove from the heat and stir in the red chile and red onion, then let cool. When cool, stir in the cucumber and set aside.

Thread the chicken onto 12 metal skewers, then cook under a preheated medium-hot broiler for 4–5 minutes on each side or until cooked through.

Transfer the skewers onto 4 serving plates and drizzle with a little of the dip. Serve with the remaining dip and lemon wedges to squeeze over the chicken.

For warm green chicken & rice salad, heat a large nonstick wok, add 3 cups cooked long-grain rice, and stir-fry over high heat for 3–4 minutes, until piping hot. Remove from the heat. Stir in 3 cups diced, cooked chicken breasts, 1 seeded and finely chopped red chile, and a large handful each of chopped mint and cilantro. Transfer to a large bowl, squeeze with the juice of 1 lime, season, and toss to mix well. **Total cooking time 10 minutes.**

thai-style chicken patties

Serves **4**
Total cooking time **30 minutes**

1 lb **ground chicken**
12 oz **raw peeled jumbo shrimp**
1½ inch length of trimmed **lemon grass stalk**, finely chopped
1 cup chopped **fresh cilantro**
⅓ cup chopped **mint**
1 tablespoon peeled and grated **fresh ginger root**
2 large **garlic cloves**, crushed
1 **red chile,** seeded and finely chopped
1 tablespoon **medium curry powder**
8 oz **dried rice noodles**
2 tablespoons **sunflower oil**, for brushing
salt and **black pepper**

To serve
lime wedges
sweet chili dipping sauce

Put the chicken, shrimp, lemon grass, chopped herbs, ginger, garlic, red chile, and curry powder into a food processor or blender and process until fairly smooth. Using wet hands, divide the mixture into 12 portions and shape each portion into a patty. Transfer to a nonstick baking sheet, cover, and chill for 8–10 minutes.

Meanwhile, cook the rice noodles according to the package directions, then drain and keep warm.

Brush the patties with oil and season. Cook under a preheated medium-hot broiler for about 10 minutes, turning once or twice, or until browned and just cooked through.

Transfer the patties to 4 serving plates and serve with the rice noodles, lime wedges, and a sweet chili dipping sauce.

For chicken, shrimp & lemon grass stir-fry, heat 2 tablespoons sunflower oil in a large wok or skillet until hot, add 1 lb ground chicken, 1 tablespoon green curry paste, and 1 tablespoon lemon grass paste, and stir-fry over high heat for 3–4 minutes or until sealed and browned. Stir in 10 oz cooked peeled shrimp, 1 tablespoon light soy sauce, and 1 tablespoon Thai fish sauce and heat for 3–4 minutes, until piping hot. Serve with noodles. **Total cooking time 10 minutes.**

curried chicken samosas

Serves **4**

Total cooking time **30 minutes**

2 **russet potatoes**, peeled
 and finely chopped
1 cup **frozen mixed
 vegetables,** such as
 peas, corn, and carrots
1½ cups chopped **cooked
 chicken**
1 tablespoon **medium
 curry paste**
1 tablespoon **mango chutney,**
 plus extra to serve
8 sheets of **phyllo pastry,**
 thawed if frozen, folded
 in half
1 tablespoon **sunflower oil**
1 tablespoon **poppy seeds**

Cook the potatoes in a saucepan of lightly salted boiling water for 5 minutes, adding the frozen vegetables toward the end so that they thaw.

Meanwhile, mix together the chicken, curry paste, and mango chutney. Drain the vegetables, add to the chicken, and mix well.

Place 2 tablespoons of the mixture in the corner of a folded sheet of phyllo pastry. Fold the end of the pastry over the filling to make a triangle, then continue folding along the pastry, keeping the triangular shape until the pastry is used up. Place on a baking sheet and repeat with remaining filling and pastry to make 8 samosas.

Brush the tops of the samosas with oil, sprinkle with poppy seeds, and bake in a preheated oven, at 400°F, for 15 minutes, until golden and crisp. Serve with mango chutney.

For curried chicken & rice, mix together 1 cup cooked basmati or other long-grain rice with 1 tablespoon medium curry paste and 1 tablespoon mango chutney. Add 1½ cups chopped cooked chicken and 1 cup frozen mixed vegetables. Heat in a microwave oven for 5 minutes, until hot. Serve with extra mango chutney and flatbreads. **Total cooking time 10 minutes.**

piquant chicken brochettes

Serves **4**
Total cooking time **20 minutes**

1¼ lb **boneless, skinless
chicken breasts**, cut into
bite-size pieces
finely grated zest and juice
of 1 **lemon**
1 **red chile,** seeded and finely
chopped
1 teaspoon **hot smoked
paprika**
½ cup **extra virgin olive oil**
1 tablespoon **dried oregano**
3 **garlic cloves**, crushed
1 **onion**, cut into large pieces
1 **red bell pepper**, cored,
seeded, and cut into large
pieces
1 **yellow bell pepper**, cored,
seeded, and cut into large
pieces
salt and **black pepper**

Put the chicken into a shallow, nonreactive bowl.
Mix together the lemon zest and juice, chile, smoked
paprika, oil, oregano, and garlic in a bowl, then season
well. Pour the mixture over the chicken and toss to
coat evenly.

Thread the chicken onto 8 metal skewers, alternating
with the onion and red and yellow bell peppers. Cook
under a preheated medium-hot broiler for 4–5 minutes
on each side or until the chicken is cooked through.

Transfer the brochettes to 4 serving plates and serve
with lemon wedges to squeeze over the top, if desired.

For piquant chicken & mixed pepper salad, put
4 coarsely shredded cooked chicken breasts, 1 (12 oz)
jar mixed roasted peppers, drained, and a handful of
arugula in a large salad bowl. Mix together 1 teaspoon
chili paste, ⅓ cup extra virgin olive oil, 1 teaspoon honey,
and the juice of 1 large lemon in a bowl, then season.
Pour the dressing over the salad, toss to mix well, and
serve. **Total cooking time 10 minutes.**

spicy chicken crepes

Serves **4**

Total cooking time **20 minutes**

2 tablespoons **butter**, plus
  extra for greasing
4 cups sliced **baby
  cremini mushrooms**
6 **scallions**, finely sliced
2 **garlic cloves**, crushed
1 tablespoon **hot curry
  powder**
1 **red chile,** seeded and sliced
2 cups **prepared four
  cheese sauce**
2 (5 oz) packages **baby
  spinach**
2 **cooked chicken breasts,**
  shredded
¼ cup chopped **fresh cilantro**
8 **cooked crepes** (prepared
  from a pancake mix, adding a
  little extra liquid for a thinner
  consistency, thawed if frozen)
½ cup grated **Parmesan
  cheese**
salt and **black pepper**
mixed salad, to serve

Heat the butter in a large skillet, add the mushrooms, scallions, garlic, curry powder, and red chile and cook over high heat for 4–5 minutes, stirring frequently, until the mushrooms are softened. Stir in half of the cheese sauce and heat until just simmering. Add the spinach and cook for 1 minute or until just wilted. Remove from the heat, stir in the chicken and cilantro, and season.

Place 1 crepe on a clean work surface and spoon one-eighth of the mushroom and spinach mixture down the center. Carefully roll the crepe up and put into a shallow greased gratin dish. Repeat with the remaining crepes.

Drizzle the remaining cheese sauce over the crepes, sprinkle with the Parmesan, and season. Cook under a preheated medium-hot broiler for 3–4 minutes or until piping hot and golden. Serve with a mixed salad.

For chicken, mushroom & spinach salad with spicy yogurt dressing, put 4 shredded cooked chicken breasts, 1 (6 oz) package baby spinach, and 3 cups thinly sliced white button mushrooms into a salad bowl. Mix together 1¼ cups plain yogurt with 1 tablespoon mild curry powder, 2 tablespoons chopped fresh cilantro, and the juice of 1 lemon in a bowl, then season. Drizzle the dressing over the salad, toss to mix well, and serve. **Total cooking time 10 minutes.**

vietnamese herb chicken rice

Serves **4**
Total cooking time **30 minutes**

2 cups **long-grain rice**, rinsed
   and drained
3½ cups **chicken broth**
1 lb **boneless, skinless**
   chicken thighs, sliced
6 **shallots**, finely sliced
2 **red chiles**, finely sliced
2 teaspoons peeled and
   grated **fresh ginger root**
handful of **mint**, chopped
handful of **fresh cilantro**,
   chopped
8 **scallions**, finely sliced

Nuoc cham sauce
2 **garlic cloves**, chopped
1 **red chile**, chopped
1 **lime**
3–4 tablespoons **Thai**
   fish sauce
1–2 tablespoons **water**

Make the nuoc cham sauce. Put the garlic and red chile into a mortar and mash with the pestle to form a paste. Squeeze the juice of the lime into the paste, then remove the pulp and add it to the mixture. Mash to a paste again, then stir in enough fish sauce and water to dilute. Set aside.

Put the rice into a heavy saucepan, then stir in the broth, chicken, shallots, red chiles, and ginger and bring to a boil. Cover tightly, reduce the heat to low, and cook, undisturbed, for 12–15 minutes or until the liquid is absorbed, the rice is tender, and the chicken is cooked through.

Remove the pan from the heat and stir in the herbs and scallions. Cover and let stand for a few minutes.

Ladle into warm bowls and serve with the nuoc cham sauce spooned over the chicken and rice or in a bowl on the side.

For Vietnamese chicken, herb & rice salad, put 2½ cups cooked basmati or other long-grain rice, 3 cups shredded, cooked chicken breasts, 1 shredded cucumber, 1 finely chopped red chile, and a small handful each of chopped mint and cilantro into a large salad bowl. Make the nuoc cham sauce as above, then spoon 2 tablespoons over the salad. Toss to mix well and serve. **Total cooking time 10 minutes.**

spiced chicken stew

Serves **4**
Total cooking time **30 minutes**

2 tablespoons **olive oil**
1 ¼ lb **boneless, skinless chicken breasts**, cut into bite-size pieces
1 large **onion**, thinly sliced
4 **garlic cloves**, finely chopped
1 teaspoon peeled and finely grated **fresh ginger root**
1 **red chile**, seeded and finely chopped
2 teaspoons **ground cumin**
3 **cinnamon sticks**
¼ teaspoon **ground turmeric**
2 large **carrots**, peeled and cut into bite-size pieces
large pinch of **saffron threads**
3 cups hot **chicken broth**
1 tablespoon **rose harissa paste**
8 **green olives**, pitted
8 **black ripe olives**, pitted
6 small **preserved lemons**, halved
salt and **black pepper**

Heat the oil in a large, heavy saucepan, add the chicken and onion, and cook over high heat for 2–3 minutes, stirring occasionally, until browned. Add the garlic, ginger, red chile, cumin, cinnamon sticks, and turmeric and cook, stirring, for 30 seconds.

Stir in the carrots, saffron, and broth and bring to a boil. Reduce the heat to medium and cook, uncovered, for 15–20 minutes or until the chicken is cooked through and the carrots are tender.

Add the harissa, olives, and preserved lemons, season, and stir to mix well. Ladle into warm bowls and serve immediately.

For spicy lemon chicken salad, put 4 coarsely shredded cooked chicken breasts and the leaves from 1 romaine lettuce into a large serving dish. Mix together the juice of 1 lemon, 2 tablespoons finely chopped preserved lemons, 2 teaspoons harissa paste, 1 tablespoon honey, and ⅓ cup olive oil in a bowl. Season and serve with the salad. **Total cooking time 10 minutes**.

sweet & spicy chicken noodles

Serves **4**

Total cooking time **20 minutes**

12 oz **dried medium egg noodles**

2 tablespoons **sunflower oil**

12 oz **boneless, skinless chicken breasts**, cubed

1 (12 oz) package **prepared stir-fry vegetables**

2 **red chiles**, seeded and sliced

1 **garlic clove**, crushed

1 tablespoon **cornstarch**

⅓ cup **light soy sauce**

⅓ cup **sweet chili sauce**

1 tablespoon **rice wine vinegar**

¼ cup **tomato puree** or **sauce**

1 tablespoon packed **light brown sugar**

½ teaspoon **ground ginger**

¼ cup **water**

1 cup small **pineapple pieces**

4 **scallions**, thinly sliced

Cook the noodles according to the package directions, then drain and keep warm.

Meanwhile, heat the oil in a large wok or skillet until hot, add the chicken, and stir-fry over medium-high heat for 6–8 minutes or until lightly browned and just cooked through. Add the stir-fry vegetables and stir-fry for another 3–4 minutes.

Mix together the red chiles, garlic, cornstarch, soy sauce, chili sauce, vinegar, tomato puree or sauce, sugar, and ground ginger in a small bowl. Add this mixture to the wok with the measured water, pineapple, and scallions and stir-fry for 2–3 minutes or until all the ingredients are well coated.

Add the reserved noodles to the wok, toss to mix well, and heat until piping hot. Divide into warm bowls and serve immediately.

For sweet & spicy chicken & pea rice, heat

2 tablespoons sunflower oil in a large wok until hot, add 2½ cups cooked rice, 2 cups frozen peas, 1 tablespoon sweet chili sauce, ¼ cup light soy sauce, 1 tablespoon garlic paste, and 1 tablespoon ginger paste, and stir-fry over high heat for 4–5 minutes. Add 3 cups diced cooked chicken breasts and stir-fry for 2–3 minutes or until piping hot. **Total cooking time 10 minutes.**

harissa chicken

Serves **4**
Total cooking time **30 minutes**

3 tablespoons **olive oil**
1 large **onion**, coarsely
  chopped
1 lb **boneless, skinless**
  chicken breasts, sliced
½ teaspoon **ground**
  cinnamon
1 teaspoon **ground cumin**
1 teaspoon **ground coriander**
2 tablespoons **harissa**
1 (14½ oz) can **diced**
  tomatoes
⅔ cup hot **chicken broth**
1 (15 oz) can **chickpeas**
  (garbanzo beans), rinsed
  and drained
couscous, to serve

Heat the oil in a large, heavy wok or skillet, add the chopped onion and sliced chicken, and cook over high heat for 5 minutes. Add the spices and cook, stirring, for 2 minutes.

Add the harissa and continue to cook for another 2 minutes before adding the diced tomatoes and broth. Bring to a boil, reduce the heat, cover, and gently simmer for 15 minutes, stirring occasionally.

Stir in the drained chickpeas (garbanzo beans) and cook for another 2 minutes, until piping hot. Serve with couscous.

For yogurt & harissa chicken kebabs, cut 1 lb boneless, skinless chicken breasts into cubes and put them into a bowl with ¼ cup plain yogurt, 1 tablespoon harissa, a pinch each of cinnamon, cumin, and coriander, and 2 tablespoons chopped fresh cilantro. Toss well to coat the chicken. Thread onto 4 metal skewers and place on an aluminum foil-lined broiler rack with 12 cherry tomatoes. Broil the kebabs and cherry tomatoes for 8–10 minutes, turning once, or until lightly charred and cooked through. Serve with couscous. **Total cooking time 20 minutes.**

curried chicken & peas

Serves **4**

Total cooking time **30 minutes**

3 tablespoons **vegetable oil**

2 teaspoons **cumin seeds**

2 **onions**, finely chopped

1 tablespoon peeled and
grated **fresh ginger root**

1 tablespoon grated **garlic**

1 lb **ground chicken**

2 tablespoons **ground
coriander**

1 teaspoon **hot chili powder**

1 tablespoon **ground cumin**

1 tablespoon **garam masala**

1 **red bell pepper**, cored,
seeded, and finely chopped

⅔ cup **frozen peas**

2 **ripe tomatoes**, finely
chopped

juice of ½ **lime**

chopped **fresh cilantro
leaves**, to garnish

To serve

chapatis or other **flatbreads**,
warmed

plain yogurt

Heat the oil in a large wok or skillet until hot, add
the cumin seeds, and stir-fry over medium heat for
1 minute. Add the onions and stir-fry for another
3–4 minutes, until softened, then add the ginger and
garlic and continue to stir-fry for 1 minute.

Add the ground chicken and the ground spices and
stir-fry for 5–7 minutes or until sealed and lightly
browned. Stir in the red bell pepper, peas, and tomatoes
and stir-fry for another 3–4 minutes or until cooked
through and piping hot.

Remove from the heat and stir in the lime juice. Spoon
into warm bowls, sprinkle with chopped cilantro, and
serve with warm chapatis or other flatbreads and a
dollop of yogurt, sprinkled with a little garam masala.

For quick chicken & pea curry, heat 2 tablespoons
olive oil in a large wok until hot, add 1¼ lb ground
chicken and 2 tablespoons green curry paste, and stir-
fry over high heat for 3–4 minutes or until the chicken
is cooked through. Stir in 1¾ cups coconut milk and
⅔ cup frozen peas and cook for another 3–4 minutes.
Season well, then serve with jasmine rice or crusty
bread. **Total cooking time 10 minutes.**

cold chicken with salsa verde

Serves **4**

Total cooking time **10 minutes**

1 **cooked roasted chicken**
(about 3 lb)

Spicy salsa verde

2 tablespoons **red wine
vinegar**

⅔ cup chopped **flat leaf
parsley**

½ cup chopped **basil** or **mint**

2 **garlic cloves**, crushed

2 **red chiles**, seeded and finely
chopped

4 **anchovy fillets in oil**,
drained and chopped

2 tablespoons **salted capers**,
rinsed

½ cup **extra virgin olive oil**,
plus extra if needed

black pepper

Make the spicy salsa verde. Pour the vinegar into the bowl of a mini food processor, then add the herbs and pulse to form a coarse paste. Add the garlic, red chiles, anchovies, and capers and process again to a coarse paste. Gradually add the oil through the feed tube with the motor still running, but do not overprocess. Season with black pepper.

Cut up the chicken and transfer to 4 plates. Spoon the spicy salsa verde over the chicken pieces and serve.

For poached chicken with spicy salsa verde, put 4 large boneless, skinless chicken breasts into a large saucepan and pour 3½ cups hot chicken broth over them. Add 1 bay leaf, 1 chopped carrot, 2 chopped celery sticks, and 1 quartered onion. Bring to a boil, then reduce the heat to medium and cook, uncovered, for 20 minutes or until the chicken is cooked through. Meanwhile, make the salsa verde as above. Remove the chicken from the pan with a slotted spoon and drain on paper towels. Slice the chicken and serve with the salsa verde. **Total cooking time 30 minutes.**

chicken with spicy arugula pesto

Serves **4**

Total cooking time **30 minutes**

16–20 **small tomatoes on the vine** (about 1 ¼ lb)

olive oil, for brushing

4 large **boneless, skinless chicken breasts**

salt and **black pepper**

Pesto

4 **garlic cloves**, crushed

2 **red chiles**, seeded and finely chopped

¾ cup **basil**

1 ½ cups **arugula leaves**

½ cup grated **Parmesan cheese**

¾ cup **pine nuts**, toasted

⅔ cup **extra virgin olive oil**, plus extra if needed

Brush the tomatoes with olive oil and season well. Put onto a nonstick baking sheet and cook in a preheated oven, at 425°F, for 10–12 minutes.

Meanwhile, lay a chicken breast between 2 sheets of plastic wrap and flatten slightly with a rolling pin or meat mallet. Repeat with the remaining chicken breasts. Brush lightly with oil and season. Heat a ridged grill pan until smoking hot, add the chicken, and cook for 5–6 minutes on each side or until cooked through. Remove the chicken and let rest for 2–3 minutes.

While the chicken is cooking, make the pesto. Put all the ingredients into a food processor or blender and process until fairly smooth, adding a little more oil for a runnier consistency, if desired.

Transfer the chicken to 4 warm serving plates, drizzle with the pesto, and serve with the roasted tomatoes.

For chicken salad with spicy arugula pesto, make the pesto as above. Put 4 thinly sliced, cooked chicken breasts and 8 halved small tomatoes into a salad bowl. Drizzle with the pesto, toss to mix well, and serve. **Total cooking time 10 minutes.**

spicy vietnamese chicken

Serves **4**
Total cooking time **20 minutes**

3 tablespoons **sunflower oil**
1¼ lb **boneless, skinless chicken breasts**, cut into strips
12 **scallions**, cut into 1 inch lengths
4 **garlic cloves**, finely chopped
1 **red chile,** seeded and finely sliced
2 **star anise**
3 inch length of trimmed **lemon grass stalk,** finely chopped
1 teaspoon crushed **cardamom seeds**
1 **cinnamon stick**
3 cups sliced **snow peas**
1 **carrot**, peeled and cut into batons
2 tablespoons **Thai fish sauce**
3 tablespoons **oyster sauce**

To garnish
handful of **fresh cilantro,** chopped
handful of **mint**, chopped
chopped **roasted peanuts**

Heat half the oil in a large wok or skillet until hot, add the chicken, and stir-fry over high heat for 3–4 minutes or until lightly browned and just cooked through. Remove with a slotted spoon and keep warm.

Heat the remaining oil in the wok or pan until hot, add the scallions, and stir-fry for 1–2 minutes, until softened. Add the garlic, red chile, star anise, lemon grass, cardamom, cinnamon stick, snow peas, and carrot and stir-fry for another 3–4 minutes or until the vegetables are softened.

Return the chicken to the wok or pan with the fish sauce and oyster sauce and continue to stir-fry for 3–4 minutes or until the chicken is cooked through and piping hot.

Spoon into warm bowls, sprinkle with chopped herbs and peanuts, and serve immediately.

For Vietnamese chicken soup, put 3½ cups chicken broth, 1 tablespoon lemon grass paste, 1 teaspoon chili paste, 1 teaspoon garlic paste, and 1 teaspoon ground cinnamon into a saucepan and bring to a boil. Stir in 3 cups shredded cooked chicken breasts and cook for 1–2 minutes or until piping hot. **Total cooking time 10 minutes.**

thai red curry with chicken balls

Serves **4**

Total cooking time **30 minutes**

1 lb **ground chicken**

1 tablespoon **lemon grass paste**

1 teaspoon **minced ginger paste**

½ cup chopped **fresh cilantro**

1 small **red Thai chile,** finely chopped

1 tablespoon **vegetable oil**

2 tablespoons **red Thai curry paste**

1¾ cups **coconut milk**

salt and **black pepper**

Put the chicken into a large bowl with the lemon grass paste, ginger paste, 3 tablespoons of the chopped fresh cilantro, and the chopped red chile. Season well with a little salt and black pepper and mix well with a fork to blend the spices into the chicken. Shape the mixture into 32 walnut-size balls.

Heat the oil in a large, heavy skillet and cook the meatballs over high heat for 8–10 minutes, in batches if necessary, until golden in places, lightly shaking the pan to turn the meatballs. Mix the curry paste into the coconut milk and pour it over the meatballs. Bring to a boil, then reduce the heat and simmer for 5 minutes, until the chicken balls are cooked through. Stir in the remaining fresh cilantro and serve with boiled rice, if desired.

For Thai chicken burgers, put 12 oz ground chicken into a bowl with 1 tablespoon Thai curry paste and 3 tablespoons chopped fresh cilantro. Shape the meat into 4 patty shapes and flatten as much as possible without the patties breaking. Heat 1 tablespoon vegetable oil in a large, heavy skillet and cook the patties for 2–3 minutes on each side over high heat until golden and cooked through. Serve the burgers in hamburger buns with salad. **Total cooking time 10 minutes.**

144

chicken biryani

Serves **4**

Total cooking time **30 minutes**

1 ½ cups **quick-cooking basmati** or other **long-grain rice**

2 tablespoons **vegetable oil**

1 **large onion**, thinly sliced

2 **boneless, skinless chicken breasts,** diced

1 **bay leaf**

3 **cardamom pods**

1 teaspoon ground **turmeric**

¼ cup **curry paste**

⅔ cup **chicken broth**

½ cup **raisins**

¼ cup **plain yogurt**

½ cup **toasted slivered almonds**

¼ cup chopped **fresh cilantro,** to garnish

Cook the rice in a large saucepan of lightly salted boiling water for 15–20 minutes, or according to the package directions, until tender.

Meanwhile, heat the oil in a large, heavy skillet, add the onion and chicken, and cook over medium-high heat for 5–8 minutes or until golden, adding the bay leaf, cardamom, and turmeric for the final 1 minute of cooking.

Add the curry paste and stir-fry for 1 minute, then pour in the broth. Bring to a boil, add the raisins and yogurt, and cook gently for 10 minutes, until the broth has reduced by half.

Drain the cooked rice, add to the pan with the chicken, and toss and cook for 2–3 minutes. Sprinkle with slivered almonds and garnish with chopped fresh cilantro.

For simple fruity chicken biryani, prepare 1 (9 oz) package precooked rice according to the package directions and set aside. Heat 1 tablespoon vegetable oil in a heavy skillet and cook 2 diced boneless, skinless chicken breasts over high heat for 8 minutes or until golden and cooked through. Add 2 tablespoons curry paste, ½ cup raisins, and ¼ cup slivered almonds and toss well in the pan. Add the cooked rice and toss again before garnishing with fresh cilantro to serve. **Total cooking time 10 minutes.**

spicy chicken risotto

Serves **4**

Total cooking time **30 minutes**

4 tablespoons **butter**

1 tablespoon **olive oil**

1 **onion**, finely chopped

1 **red chile,** seeded and finely chopped

2 **garlic cloves**, finely chopped

1 **celery stick**, finely chopped

1 **carrot**, peeled and finely chopped

1½ cups **risotto rice**

½ cup **dry white wine**

3 **cooked chicken breasts**, diced

4 cups hot **vegetable broth**

1 cup finely grated **Parmesan cheese**

finely grated zest of **1 lemon**

⅓ cup finely chopped **tarragon**

salt and **black pepper**

Heat the butter and oil in a large skillet, add the onion, chile, garlic, celery, and carrot, and cook over medium heat for 3–4 minutes, until softened. Add the rice and stir for 1 minute or until the grains are well coated. Pour in the wine and stir until it has been absorbed, then stir in the chicken.

Add 1 ladle of hot broth and simmer, stirring, until it has been absorbed. Repeat with another ladle of broth, then reserve 1 ladle and continue to add the remaining broth at intervals and cook as before for another 18–20 minutes or until the liquid has been absorbed and the rice is tender but still firm ("al dente").

Stir in the reserved broth, Parmesan, lemon zest, and tarragon, season, and mix well. Remove from the heat, cover, and let stand for 2 minutes.

Spoon into warm bowls, season, and serve immediately.

For chicken, lemon & tarragon baguettes, slice
2 warm medium baguettes into half horizontally and spread each with 2 tablespoons prepared tarragon mayonnaise. Divide 2 sliced cooked chicken breasts between the baguette bottoms, then sprinkle with the finely grated zest of ½ lemon and season. Top with the baguette lids, then cut each into 2 and serve. **Total cooking time 10 minutes.**

chicken & mango noodles

Serves **4**

Total cooking time **10 minutes**

2 tablespoons **vegetable oil**

2 tablespoons **hot chili sauce**

¼ cup **sweet chili sauce**

¼ cup **dark soy sauce**

2 large **skinless chicken breasts**, cut into thin strips

1⅓ cups **fresh mango chunks**

1 (12 oz) package **prepared stir-fry vegetables**

1 lb **medium egg noodles, cooked**

½ cup **dry-roasted peanuts,** chopped

salt and **black pepper**

Mix together the oil, hot chili sauce, sweet chili sauce, and soy sauce in a large bowl. Add the chicken strips, season, and mix together.

Heat a large nonstick wok or skillet until hot, then add the chicken, reserving the marinade, and stir-fry over high heat for 5 minutes or until lightly browned and cooked through. Add the mango, stir-fry vegetables, noodles, and the reserved marinade and stir-fry for another few minutes, until piping hot.

Mix in the chopped peanuts, then divide among 4 warm bowls. Serve immediately.

For spicy chicken & mango skewers, cut 4 large boneless, skinless chicken breasts into bite-size pieces and put into a bowl with 1 tablespoon hot chili sauce, 2 tablespoons sweet chili sauce, and 2 tablespoons light soy sauce. Stir to mix well. Thread the chicken onto 12 metal skewers, alternating with 2½ cups fresh mango chunks. Cook under a preheated medium-hot broiler for 4–5 minutes on each side or until the chicken is cooked through. Serve with a mixed leaf salad. **Total cooking time 20 minutes.**

thai green coconut chicken

Serves **4**

Total cooking time **30 minutes**

4 large **boneless chicken
breasts**, skin on
1 teaspoon **Thai green curry
paste**
¼ cup **coconut milk**
2 tablespoons **fresh white
bread crumbs**
finely grated zest of **1 lime**
1 teaspoon **lemon grass
paste**
sunflower oil, for drizzling
salt and **black pepper**

To serve
steamed **jasmine rice**
steamed **Chinese greens**

Using a small, sharp knife, cut a slit down the side of each chicken breast to form a deep pocket. Mix together the remaining ingredients in a bowl, then season well. Divide the mixture evenly among the 4 chicken pockets.

Drizzle with a little oil, then transfer to a nonstick baking sheet. Place in a preheated oven, at 350°F, for 18–20 minutes or until the chicken is cooked through.

Serve with steamed jasmine rice and Chinese greens.

For quick Thai green chicken curry, heat 2 tablespoons sunflower oil in a large wok or skillet until hot, add 2 tablespoons Thai green curry paste, and stir-fry over medium heat for 1–2 minutes. Stir in 4 diced cooked chicken breasts and 1¾ cups coconut milk and bring to a boil. Cook for 3–4 minutes or until piping hot, then remove from the heat, season, and stir in ¼ cup each of chopped fresh cilantro and Thai basil leaves. Serve with steamed rice or noodles. **Total cooking time 10 minutes.**

family
favorites

honey & mustard chicken salad

Serves **4**

Total cooking time **20 minutes**

3 tablespoons **extra virgin olive oil**

1 teaspoon **honey**

1 teaspoon **Dijon mustard**

1 teaspoon **lemon juice**

3 **boneless, skinless chicken breasts**

2 tablespoons **pumpkin seeds**

4 cups **mixed peppery salad greens**

1 ⅓ cups **frozen peas**, thawed

1 large **avocado**, pitted, peeled, pitted, and cut into slices

Whisk together the olive oil, honey, mustard, and lemon juice in a small bowl to make a dressing.

Place the chicken breasts on an aluminum foil-lined baking sheet. Cook under a preheated hot broiler for 5–6 minutes on each side or until cooked through.

Meanwhile, heat a small, nonstick skillet over medium heat, add the pumpkin seeds, and dry-fry until golden, stirring frequently. Remove from the pan and set aside.

Divide the mixed peppery salad greens among 4 plates.

Slice the chicken diagonally and divide among the plates of salad greens. Sprinkle with the peas, avocado, and pumpkin seeds, pour the dressing over the salad, and serve immediately.

For chicken, avocado & mustard sandwiches,

spread 4 slices of bread with 1 teaspoon whole-grain mustard. Divide 1 cup peppery salad greens among the slices of bread, then top with 2 sliced honey-roasted chicken breasts and 1 large pitted, peeled, and sliced avocado. Top with 4 more slices of bread to make 4 sandwiches. **Total cooking time 10 minutes.**

mexican chicken burgers

Serves **2**
Total cooking time **20 minutes**

2 **boneless, skinless chicken breasts** (about 5 oz each), halved horizontally
2 teaspoons **fajita seasoning**
1 tablespoon **olive oil**
1 **red bell pepper**, cored, quartered, and seeded
2 tablespoons **sour cream**
chopped **chives**
2 **hamburger buns**, halved
½ **avocado**, pitted, peeled, and sliced

Tomato salad
5 **cherry tomatoes**, halved
½ small **red onion**, thinly sliced
½ **red chile**, seeded and chopped
1 tablespoon chopped **flat leaf parsley**
squeeze of **lime juice**
salt and **black pepper**

Coat the chicken pieces in fajita seasoning, put onto an aluminum foil-lined broiler rack, and drizzle with the oil, then add the bell pepper quarters, skin side up, to the broiler rack. Cook under a preheated medium broiler for 10–15 minutes, turning occasionally, until the chicken is cooked through and the bell peppers are soft and lightly charred.

Meanwhile, make the salad. Mix together all the ingredients in a bowl and season.

Mix together the sour cream and chives in a small bowl.

Toast the hamburger buns, then fill with the avocado slices, chicken, and broiled bell peppers. Top with spoonfuls of tomato salad and sour cream. Serve with the remaining tomato salad.

For loaded chicken nachos, spread out 1 (7 oz) package tortilla chips in an ovenproof dish. Sprinkle with 1 cup chopped cooked barbecue chicken. Top with 2 tablespoons tomato salsa. Add 1 tablespoon sliced jalapeño peppers from a jar and sprinkle with ¾ cup shredded cheddar cheese. Cook under a preheated hot broiler for 3–4 minutes, until melted and warm. Serve with prepared guacamole. **Total cooking time 10 minutes.**

baked chicken with lime

Serves **4**

Total cooking time **30 minutes**

2 **limes**

1 inch piece of **fresh ginger root**, peeled and finely grated

1 teaspoon **Thai fish sauce**

1 tablespoon **peanut** or **vegetable oil**

large bunch of **fresh cilantro**

4 **boneless, skinless chicken breasts** (about 5 oz each)

2 cups **jasmine rice**, rinsed

2½ cups cold **water**

salt

Finely grate the zest from the 2 limes, squeeze the juice from one of them, and finely slice the other.

Put the lime zest and juice into a mini chopper with the ginger, fish sauce, oil, and cilantro, including the stems. Blend to make a paste.

Cut 3 deep slashes diagonally into the chicken breasts and massage the paste all over the chicken. Put a slice of lime into each slash.

Put the chicken breasts into a roasting pan, cover with aluminum foil, and bake in a preheated oven, at 400°F, for 18–20 minutes or until the chicken is cooked through.

Meanwhile, put the rice into a large saucepan with the measured water, season with salt, and bring to a boil. Reduce the heat, cover with a tight-fitting lid, and cook gently for 15–18 minutes, or according to the package directions, until all of the water has been absorbed and the rice is tender and sticky. Serve the chicken with the sticky rice, drizzled with chicken juices.

For chicken & lime noodle salad, put 1 lb rice noodles, cooked and cooled, into a serving bowl with 2 cups cooked chicken strips, the grated zest of 1 lime, a bunch of cilantro, chopped, and 1 thinly sliced red bell pepper, then toss to combine. Pour 3 tablespoons vegetable oil into a small bowl with 2 tablespoons lime juice, 2 teaspoons grated fresh ginger root, and 1 tablespoon Thai fish sauce and whisk to combine. Drizzle the salad with the dressing to serve. **Total cooking time 10 minutes.**

pasta with chili chicken sauce

Serves **4**

Total cooking time **20 minutes**

1 tablespoon **sunflower oil**
1 lb **ground chicken**
1 **garlic clove**, crushed
1 teaspoon **chili powder**
½ teaspoon **dried red
  pepper flakes**
2 cups **tomato puree**
  or **sauce**
1 tablespoon **tomato pesto**
1 lb **spaghetti**
salt and **black pepper**
freshly grated **Parmesan
  cheese**, to serve

Heat the oil in a large skillet, add the ground chicken, and cook over high heat for 5 minutes, breaking up any clumps.

Add the garlic, chili powder, red pepper flakes, tomato puree or sauce, and pesto. Season with salt and black pepper, bring to a boil, then reduce the heat and simmer for 10 minutes.

Meanwhile, cook the spaghetti in a saucepan of lightly salted boiling water for 8–10 minutes, or according to the package directions, until "al dente." Drain and toss with the chicken chili sauce. Serve with plenty of freshly grated Parmesan cheese.

For baked spicy chicken, cut several slashes across the top of 4 boneless chicken breasts (with skin on). Put into an aluminum foil-lined baking pan and pour over a mixture of ⅓ cup balsamic vinegar, 2 tablespoons lemon juice, ¼ cup olive oil, and 1 chopped red chile. Bake in a preheated oven, at 400°F, for 25 minutes with 1 (16 oz) package frozen roasted potatoes in a separate baking pan until the chicken is cooked through and the potatoes are crisp. Serve with peas. **Total cooking time 30 minutes.**

chicken & tarragon burgers

Serves **4**

Total cooking time **20 minutes**

1 lb **boneless, skinless chicken breasts**, coarsely chopped

1 tablespoon **whole-grain mustard**

3 tablespoons chopped **tarragon**

½ small **red chile,** finely chopped (optional)

4 **whole wheat hamburger buns**

black pepper

To serve

bearnaise sauce from a jar

arugula tossed in **lemon juice**

Put the chicken into a food processor and process until smooth. Transfer to a bowl, add the mustard, tarragon, and chile, if using, and season well with black pepper. Mix together until well blended, then shape into 4 patties.

Lay the chicken patties on an aluminum foil-lined broiler rack and cook under a preheated hot broiler for 4–5 minutes on each side, until browned and cooked through. Halve the buns and place, cut side up, under the broiler for the final 1 minute of cooking time.

Place a hot burger on the top of each warm bun bottom and top with a spoonful of bearnaise sauce and a handful of lemon juice-dressed arugula. Cover with the warm bun tops and serve immediately.

For crunchy chicken burgers with tarragon mayonnaise, place 4 boneless, skinless chicken breasts (about 5 oz each), between 2 sheets of lightly oiled plastic wrap and bash with a rolling pin until half their original thickness. Beat 1 egg with 1 teaspoon Dijon mustard. Put 2 cups fresh white bread crumbs into a separate bowl. Dip each chicken breast into the egg mixture and then coat in bread crumbs. Cook under a preheated broiler for 4 minutes on each side until crisp and brown. Meanwhile, stir 1 tablespoon chopped tarragon and 1 teaspoon lemon juice into ¼ cup mayonnaise. Serve on the burgers in toasted buns, with salad greens. **Total cooking time 10 minutes.**

chicken & vegetable satay

Serves **4**

Total cooking time **20 minutes**

½ cup **tamari soy sauce**

3 tablespoons **smooth peanut butter**

1 tablespoons **water**

2 **boneless, skinless chicken breasts**, cut into strips

4 large **mushrooms**, halved

1 **red bell pepper**, cored, seeded, and cut into chunks

1 **yellow bell pepper**, cored, seeded, and cut into chunks

1 **zucchini**, halved and sliced

½ **crisp firm lettuce**, shredded

2 **carrots**, shredded

¼ cup **bean sprouts**

small handful of **fresh cilantro leaves**

2 teaspoons **sesame oil**

juice of **1 lime**

2 tablespoons **sesame seeds**, toasted, to serve

Mix together the tamari, peanut butter, and measured water in a large bowl.

Toss the chicken, mushrooms, bell peppers, and zucchini in the peanut mixture and thread onto 8 satay sticks that have been soaked in water to prevent burning.

Cook under a preheated hot broiler for 12–14 minutes, turning frequently, until the chicken is cooked through.

Meanwhile, toss together the lettuce, shredded carrots, bean sprouts, and cilantro leaves with the sesame oil and lime juice.

Serve the satay with the salad, sprinkled with toasted sesame seeds.

For chicken satay with satay sauce, stir-fry 1½ cups peanuts in ½ cup vegetable oil for 1 minute, then process until smooth. Sauté 2 chopped garlic cloves and 4 chopped shallots for 30 seconds, then add 1 tablespoon tamari soy sauce, 1 teaspoon packed brown sugar, 1 diced red chile, 1¾ cups water, and the blended peanuts and simmer for 7–8 minutes to thicken. Meanwhile, broil 8 prepared chicken satay sticks for 3–4 minutes on each side until cooked through. Stir the juice of 1 lemon into the satay sauce and serve with the chicken. **Total cooking time 10 minutes.**

soy chicken & rice noodles

Serves **2**

Total cooking time **10 minutes**

8 oz **rice noodles**, cooked

2 tablespoons **soy sauce**

1 tablespoon **sesame** or **vegetable oil**

½ **red chile,** seeded and finely sliced or chopped (optional)

1 teaspoon peeled and grated **fresh ginger root**

1 cup sliced or torn **cooked chicken breast**

2 **scallions**, sliced

1 **red bell pepper,** cored, seeded, and thinly sliced, or 2 cups thinly sliced **snow peas**

Put the noodles into a colander and pour boiling water over them. Drain, then cool under cold running water. Drain well and put into a large bowl.

Whisk together the soy sauce, oil, chile, if using, and ginger and drizzle the mixture over the noodles. Toss really well to coat, then add the remaining ingredients and mix gently to combine. Pile into bowls to serve.

For soy noodles with chicken, heat 2 tablespoons vegetable oil in a skillet and cook 1 large, thinly sliced skinless chicken breast over medium-high heat for 5–6 minutes, until lightly golden and just cooked through. Add 2 cups sliced snow peas, 2 sliced scallions, a ¾ inch piece of fresh ginger root, peeled and chopped, 2 sliced garlic cloves, and ½ chopped red chile. Stir-fry for 2–3 minutes, until softened, then add 2 (7 oz) pouches precooked stir-fry noodles and stir-fry for 3 minutes, until piping hot. Pour in 2 tablespoons light soy sauce and 2 tablespoons oyster sauce, toss to coat, and pile into bowls. **Total cooking time 20 minutes.**

lemon & parsley chicken skewers

Serves **2**
Total cooking time **10 minutes**

2 **boneless, skinless chicken
 breasts**, cut into chunks
finely grated zest and juice of
 1 **lemon**
2 tablespoons **olive oil**
3 tablespoons finely chopped
 parsley
salt and **black pepper**

To serve
arugula and tomato salad
pita breads, warmed
1 cup **prepared tzatziki** or
 Greek yogurt veggie dip

Put the chicken into a nonreactive bowl with the lemon
zest and juice and the oil, and toss well to coat. Stir in
the parsley and season well.

Thread the chicken onto 4 small metal skewers and
cook under a preheated hot broiler for 8–10 minutes,
until golden and cooked through, turning once. Serve
with a simple arugula and tomato salad, warm pita
breads, and spoonfuls of tzatziki or yogurt dip.

For lemon & parsley-stuffed chicken, make a
slit lengthwise in the side of 2 boneless, skinless
chicken breasts (about 5 oz each), to form pockets.
Thinly slice ½ lemon, then stuff the chicken with the
lemon slices. Press a small bunch of parsley into the
cavities and season. Tie around each piece once with
a piece of kitchen string. Heat 1 tablespoon butter
and 1 tablespoon olive oil in a skillet, add the chicken,
and cook over medium-high heat for 7–8 minutes on
each side until golden and cooked through. Serve with
a yogurt veggie dip and a simple salad. **Total cooking
time 20 minutes.**

chicken pad thai

Serves **4**

Total cooking time **10 minutes**

3 tablespoons **vegetable oil**

1 **egg**, lightly beaten

1 **garlic clove**, crushed

2 teaspoons peeled and finely
   grated **fresh ginger root**

2 **scallions**, sliced

12 oz **rice noodles**, cooked

½ cup **bean sprouts**

2 **cooked chicken breasts**,
   torn into thin strips

2 tablespoons **Thai fish sauce**

2 teaspoons **tamarind paste**

2 teaspoons **sugar**

pinch of **chili powder**

3 tablespoons coarsely
   chopped **roasted peanuts**

handful of **fresh cilantro**,
   chopped

Heat a large wok until smoking hot. Add 1 tablespoon of the oil and swirl around the pan, then pour in the egg. Stir around the pan and cook for 1–2 minutes, until just cooked through. Remove from the wok and set aside.

Heat the remaining oil in the wok, add the garlic, ginger, and scallions, and cook for 2 minutes, until softened. Add the noodles to the pan along with the bean sprouts and chicken.

Stir in the fish sauce, tamarind paste, sugar, and chili powder and continue to cook, adding a splash of boiling water, if necessary. Heat through, then return the egg to the pan and mix in. Divide among serving bowls and sprinkle with the peanuts and cilantro to serve.

For chicken noodle soup, simmer 5 cups chicken broth with 3 tablespoons rice wine, 2 tablespoons light soy sauce, and 1 star anise for 10 minutes. Mix 12 oz ground chicken with 1 teaspoon peeled and grated fresh ginger root and 1 teaspoon soy sauce. Shape into balls and cook in the soup for 7 minutes. Add 4 oz shiitake mushrooms and cook for another 3 minutes. Stir in 2 bok choy, quartered, and cook for 1 minute. Add 1 (7 oz) package precooked rice noodles, heat through, and serve. **Total cooking time 30 minutes.**

chicken breasts with herb butter

Serves **4**

Total cooking time **25 minutes**

4 tablespoons **butter**,
  softened

grated zest of **1 lemon**

1 **garlic clove**, crushed

handful of **basil**, finely
  chopped

4 **boneless, skinless
  chicken breasts**

⅓ cup **olive oil**, plus extra
  for greasing

1 cup **dried bread crumbs**

¼ cup grated **Parmesan
  cheese**

salt and **black pepper**

Mix together the butter, lemon zest, garlic, and basil and season. Use a sharp knife to make a small horizontal slit in the side of each chicken breast to form a little pocket, making sure you don't cut all the way through the meat. Tuck some of the butter inside each breast, then smooth over to seal.

Rub 1 tablespoon of the oil over each chicken breast and season well. Put the bread crumbs onto a plate and dip each breast in the crumbs until well coated.

Transfer the chicken to a lightly greased baking pan, sprinkle with the Parmesan, drizzle with the remaining oil, and cook in a preheated oven, at 400°F, for 20 minutes or until golden and cooked through. Serve with new potatoes and green beans.

For herb chicken sandwiches, mix together ⅓ cup mayonnaise, the finely grated zest of ½ lemon, and a handful of chopped basil. Cut 4 boneless, skinless chicken breasts into slices, season, and rub with 2 tablespoons oil. Cook on a preheated ridged grill pan for 5 minutes, turning once, until seared and cooked through. Spread the mayonnaise on the cut sides of 4 halved ciabatta rolls and fill with the warm chicken and some salad greens. **Total cooking time 10 minutes.**

creamy cider chicken

Serves **4**

Total cooking time **30 minutes**

3 tablespoons **olive or
vegetable oil**

8 **boneless chicken thighs**
(about 1 ¼ lb), skin on

2–3 tablespoons
seasoned **flour**

4 oz **bacon**, chopped

1 ½ cups sliced **white button
mushrooms**

1 cup boiling **vegetable
or chicken broth**

1 cup **hard dry cider** or
apple juice

2 tablespoons **apple
cider vinegar**

¼ cup **light cream** or
crème fraîche

salt and **black pepper**

Heat 2 tablespoons of the oil in a large, deep skillet.
Dust the chicken with the seasoned flour and cook in
the pan, skin side down, for about 10 minutes, until
really golden and crisp.

Meanwhile, heat the remaining oil in a small skillet
and cook the bacon for 3–4 minutes, until golden.
Add the mushrooms and cook for another 2–3 minutes,
until softened.

Turn the chicken thighs over, then add the bacon and
mushrooms to the pan. Pour over the broth, cider or
apple juice, and apple cider vinegar, bring to a boil,
then reduce the heat and simmer gently for about
15 minutes, until the chicken is cooked through.

Arrange the chicken thighs alongside the rice, then
stir the cream into the pan. Season with salt and black
pepper, then spoon the sauce over the chicken and
serve with boiled rice.

For creamy chicken rice, heat 2 tablespoons
vegetable oil in a skillet and cook 4 oz chopped back
bacon for 3–4 minutes, until golden. Add 1 ½ cups
sliced white button mushrooms and cook for another
2–3 minutes. Add 2 cups diced cooked chicken,
2 ½ cups cooked rice, and 1 ¼ cups heavy cream or
crème fraîche, then season well and stir over the heat
for 1–2 minutes, until hot. Spoon the creamy rice into
4 bowls to serve. **Total cooking time 10 minutes.**

sweet balsamic chicken

Serves **4**

Total cooking time **20 minutes**

⅓ cup **balsamic vinegar**

4 **boneless, skinless chicken breasts** (about 5 oz each)

2 tablespoons **olive oil**

1 **onion**, thinly sliced

1 **red onion**, thinly sliced

2 tablespoons **honey**

1 tablespoon chopped **rosemary**

⅔ cup **chicken broth**

black pepper

To serve

mashed potatoes

green beans

Put the balsamic vinegar into a nonreactive bowl and season with black pepper. Make 3 small cuts in the top of each of the chicken breasts. Add the chicken to the vinegar and toss to coat. Set aside for 3–4 minutes.

Meanwhile, heat the oil in a large, heavy skillet and cook the onions over medium-high heat for 5 minutes or until soft and beginning to turn golden brown. Add the chicken, cut side down, and cook for 3 minutes. Turn the chicken over and cook for another 3 minutes.

Turn once more and add the balsamic vinegar from the bowl together with the honey and rosemary. Reduce the heat, add the broth, cover, and simmer, stirring once, for 3–4 minutes or until the chicken is cooked through. Serve the chicken on warm serving plates with the onions spooned over top. Serve with mashed potatoes and green beans.

For balsamic chicken bruschetta, thinly slice 2 boneless, skinless chicken breasts (about 5 oz each), and put into a nonreactive bowl with 3 tablespoons balsamic vinegar, 1 tablespoon honey, and ½ teaspoon dried rosemary. Toss together. Heat 1 tablespoon olive oil in a large skillet and cook the chicken over high heat for 7–8 minutes, until golden brown and cooked through. Meanwhile, slice 8 large mushrooms and add to the pan for the final 4 minutes of cooking. Lightly toast 4 diagonal slices of ciabatta, spoon the balsamic chicken and mushroom over the top of each slice, and serve warm. **Total cooking time 10 minutes.**

mango & peanut chicken salad

Serves **4**
Total cooking time **10 minutes**

2 tablespoons **sesame oil**
2 **boneless, skinless chicken breasts** (about 5 oz each), thinly sliced
5 cups **mixed salad greens**
1 large ripe **mango**, pitted, peeled, and sliced
¼ cup **chunky peanut butter**
⅓ cup **coconut milk**
2 tablespoons **sweet chili sauce**
¼ cup **water**

Heat 1 tablespoon of the sesame oil in a large, heavy skillet, add the sliced chicken, and cook over high heat for 5–6 minutes, stirring frequently, until browned and cooked through.

Meanwhile, put the mixed salad greens with the mango into a large serving bowl, drizzle with the remaining sesame oil, and toss to mix.

Add the remaining ingredients to the chicken in the skillet and cook, stirring, for 1 minute. Toss the chicken into the salad and serve while still warm.

For chicken & mango kebabs, cut 3 boneless, skinless chicken breasts (about 5 oz each), into cubes and put into a bowl with ¼ cup dark soy sauce, a ½ inch piece of fresh ginger root, peeled and chopped, and ½ teaspoon Chinese five-spice powder. Toss well to coat, cover, and let marinate for 5 minutes. Meanwhile, pit, peel, and cut 1 mango into large chunks. Toss in a bowl with 1 tablespoon sesame oil and 2 tablespoons chopped fresh cilantro. Thread the chicken and mango evenly onto 8 metal skewers. Cook the kebabs under a preheated hot broiler for 8–10 minutes, turning occasionally, until browned and cooked through. **Total cooking time 20 minutes.**

chicken & tarragon pesto penne

Serves **4**
Total cooking time **10 minutes**

12 oz **penne**
½ cup **olive oil**
1 cup grated **Parmesan
  cheese**
handful of **tarragon leaves**
½ cup **pine nuts**, toasted
1 **garlic clove**, crushed
grated zest and juice of
  1 **lemon**
3 **cooked chicken breasts**,
  sliced
4 cups **peppery salad greens**
12 **baby tomatoes**, quartered

Cook the penne in a large saucepan of boiling water for 8–9 minutes, or according to the package directions, until "al dente." Drain and refresh under cold running water, then toss with 2 tablespoons of the oil.

Meanwhile, put the Parmesan, tarragon, pine nuts, garlic, and lemon zest into a food processor and process for 1 minute. Then, while the motor is still running, gradually pour in the remaining olive oil through the feed tube to form the pesto.

Toss the pesto with the pasta, chicken, peppery salad greens, tomatoes, and lemon juice, and serve.

For chicken & tarragon tagliatelle, toss 4 boneless, skinless chicken breasts (about 5 oz each), in 2 tablespoons olive oil with 2 tablespoons chopped tarragon and black pepper. Cook the chicken breasts under a preheated hot broiler for 6–8 minutes on each side or until cooked through. Meanwhile, cook 12 oz tagliatelle for 9–12 minutes or according to the package directions. Heat 1 tablespoon olive oil in a large skillet over medium heat, add 4 chopped scallions and 12 quartered baby tomatoes, and cook for 2 minutes. Slice the chicken breasts and add to the pan. Drain the pasta and toss in the pan. Serve sprinkled with 2 tablespoons toasted pine nuts. **Total cooking time 20 minutes.**

bacon & chicken pasta

Serves **4**
Total cooking time **20 minutes**

4 small **chicken breasts**
4 oz **smoked cheese** or
   mozzarella cheese, sliced
small bunch of **basil** (optional)
8 **smoked bacon slices**
2 tablespoons **olive** or
   vegetable oil
1½ cups **mascarpone and
   tomato sauce** or other
   cheese and tomato sauce
tagliatelle or **selection of
   vegetables**, to serve

Slice the chicken breasts almost in half horizontally, then stuff each pocket with the sliced cheese and 2–3 basil leaves, if using. Wrap the bacon around the chicken breasts to seal in the stuffing.

Heat the oil in a skillet, add the chicken, and cook over medium heat for 5–6 minutes on each side or until the bacon is golden and the chicken is cooked through. Pierce the chicken with the tip of a sharp knife to check that the juices run clear, then remove from the pan and set aside to rest for 2–3 minutes.

Meanwhile, gently warm the tomato sauce in the same pan, scraping any sediment from the bottom of the pan. Serve the chicken packages with cooked tagliatelle or vegetables and the warm sauce.

For chicken, ham & cheese packages, lay out 4 soft tortilla wraps and arrange 2 slices of wafer-thin cooked chicken breast and 2 oz each of wafer-thin smoked ham and smoked cheese or mozzarella, and 1–2 drained and sliced roasted peppers in the center of each tortilla. Top each with 2–3 basil leaves (optional) and fold the curved edges of each tortilla into the center 4 times to create a square package. Heat a skillet and toast the packages, 2 at a time, for 1–2 minutes on each side. Serve hot with green salad. **Total cooking time 10 minutes.**

creamy chicken pasta

Serves **4**
Total cooking time **20 minutes**

12 oz **penne**
¼ cup **olive oil**
1 lb **boneless, skinless chicken breasts**, cut into thin strips
3 **zucchini**, cut into thin slices
1 large **onion**, thinly sliced
2 teaspoons **crushed garlic**
¼ cup **pine nuts**
finely grated zest and juice of
  2 **lemons**
½ cup chopped **tarragon**
1 cup **crème fraîche** or
  cream cheese
salt
grated **Parmesan cheese**,
  to serve

Cook the penne in a large saucepan of lightly salted boiling water for 8–10 minutes, or according to the package directions, until "al dente."

Meanwhile, heat the oil in a large skillet, add the chicken, and cook for 3–4 minutes, until starting to turn golden brown. Add the zucchini and onion and cook for another 5 minutes, until golden and the chicken is cooked through.

Add the garlic and pine nuts and cook, stirring, for 2 minutes, then add the lemon zest and juice, tarragon, and crème fraîche or cream cheese and stir well until hot but not boiling.

Drain the pasta well, then add to the sauce and toss well to coat. Serve with grated Parmesan and a simple salad, if desired.

For creamy chicken & tarragon pan-fry, heat 2 tablespoons olive oil in a large skillet, add 2 thinly sliced onions and 1 lb thinly sliced boneless, skinless chicken breasts, and cook for 5 minutes, until golden and cooked through. Add ¼ cup chopped tarragon and 2 tablespoons white wine vinegar and cook for another 1 minute, then stir in 1 cup crème fraîche or heavy cream and 2 teaspoons Dijon mustard. Serve hot. **Total cooking time 10 minutes.**

sticky lemon chicken noodles

Serves **4**

Total cooking time **10 minutes**

2 tablespoons **vegetable oil**

2 **boneless, skinless chicken
breasts** (about 5 oz each),
cut into thin strips

8 oz **baby broccoli**

2 **garlic cloves**, crushed

2 teaspoons peeled and finely
grated **fresh ginger root**

1 **red chile,** finely chopped

finely grated zest and juice
of **1 lemon**

1 tablespoon **honey**

2 teaspoons **light soy sauce**

12 oz **egg noodles**, cooked

handful of **roasted
cashew nuts**

Heat a wok until smoking hot, then pour in the oil, swirl
around the pan, and add the chicken. Cook for 1 minute,
then add the broccoli and stir-fry for 5 minutes, until the
chicken is nearly cooked through.

Add the garlic, ginger, and chile to the wok and cook
for another 1 minute. Then add the lemon zest and juice,
honey, and soy sauce and toss around the pan.

Stir in the noodles and a splash of water and cook until
heated through. Divide among 4 serving bowls, sprinkle
with the cashew nuts, and serve.

For roasted lemon chicken with broccoli, mix
together 1 teaspoon ground cumin, 1 teaspoon honey,
1 crushed garlic clove, and 3 tablespoons olive oil.
Stir in the finely grated zest of 1 lemon and a squeeze
of lemon juice and season. Put 4 boneless, skinless
chicken breasts and 8 oz baby broccoli into a roasting
pan. Pour the lemon mixture over them and toss well.
Place in a preheated oven, at 400°F, for 20 minutes or
until the chicken is cooked through. Sprinkle with some
sesame seeds and serve with boiled rice. **Total cooking
time 25 minutes.**

sticky soy-glazed drumsticks

Serves **4**

Total cooking time **30 minutes**

8 **chicken drumsticks**
2 tablespoons **honey**
2 tablespoons **olive oil**
2 tablespoons **dark soy sauce**
1 teaspoon **tomato paste**
1 tablespoon **Dijon mustard**
chopped **parsley**, to garnish

Put the drumsticks onto a cutting board and make 4 deep slashes in each one along the thick part of the meat, cutting down to the bone on both sides.

Mix together the honey, oil, soy sauce, tomato paste, and mustard in a large bowl. Toss the drumsticks in the glaze, turning to cover the meat well.

Transfer the glazed drumsticks to a roasting pan and roast in the top of a preheated oven, at 425°F, for 20–25 minutes or until the chicken is cooked through. Garnish with parsley and serve with boiled rice and a salad, if desired.

For spicy sticky soy-glazed chicken breasts, mix together the honey, oil, soy sauce, tomato paste, and mustard as above to make the glaze and add 1 finely chopped small red chile. Coat 4 boneless, skinless chicken breasts (about 5 oz each) in the glaze. Heat 1 tablespoon olive oil in a large, heavy skillet and cook the chicken over medium-high heat for 15 minutes, turning it frequently and reducing the heat a little if the glaze begins to catch on the bottom of the pan, until the chicken is cooked through. Slice the cooked chicken and serve fanned on a plate, with boiled rice and salad. **Total cooking time 20 minutes.**

stir-fried lemon chicken

Serves **2**
Total cooking time **20 minutes**

1 tablespoon **peanut oil**
2 **boneless, skinless chicken breasts**, sliced
1½ cups **broccoli florets**
1 small **red bell pepper**, seeded and coarsely chopped
2 **scallions**, thickly sliced
⅓ cup **unsalted cashew nuts**
1 tablespoon **cornstarch**
½ cup cold **water**
2 tablespoons **lemon juice**
1½ tablespoons **honey**
2 tablespoons **light soy sauce**

Heat the oil in a large wok or skillet, add the chicken, and cook over medium-high heat for 3–4 minutes, until golden. Using a slotted spoon, transfer to a plate and set aside.

Return the pan to the heat and add the broccoli, red bell pepper, and scallions. Stir-fry for 3–4 minutes, until softened.

Meanwhile, put a small saucepan over medium-low heat and toast the cashew nuts for 3–4 minutes, shaking the pan occasionally, until golden. Remove from the heat.

Blend the cornstarch in a small bowl with 1 tablespoon of the water, then mix in the remaining water plus the lemon juice, honey, and soy sauce. Add to the vegetables along with the cashew nuts. Reduce the heat to medium-low and return the chicken to the pan. Simmer for 2–3 minutes, until the chicken is cooked through and the sauce hot and thickened. Serve immediately, with steamed rice or noodles, if desired.

For crunchy lemon chicken salad, put 2 teaspoons grated lemon zest into a dish with ¾ cup dried bread crumbs. Put ⅓ cup all-purpose flour in a second dish and 1 beaten egg in a third. Dip 8 oz chicken strips first in the flour, followed by the egg, and finally in the bread crumbs until coated. Heat 2 tablespoons peanut oil in a skillet and cook the chicken for 7–8 minutes, turning occasionally, until golden and cooked through. Serve with mixed salad greens, sprinkled with 2 tablespoons toasted cashew nuts and 1 thinly sliced scallion, and desired dressing. **Total cooking time 10 minutes.**

chicken & chorizo jambalaya

Serves **4**

Total cooking time **30 minutes**

1 cup **long-grain rice**
1 tablespoon **olive oil**
1 (8 oz) piece of **chorizo sausage**, cut into chunky slices
1 **onion**, chopped
2 **boneless, skinless chicken breasts** (about 5 oz each), cut into chunks
1 **red bell pepper**, cored, seeded, and cut into chunks
1 **green bell pepper**, cored, seeded, and cut into chunks
1 **yellow bell pepper**, cored, seeded, and cut into chunks
2 **celery sticks**, chopped
1 tablespoon **cornstarch**, mixed to a paste with 2 tablespoons cold water
2½ cups **chicken broth**
1 (14½ oz) can **diced tomatoes**
salt and **black pepper**
¼ cup chopped **parsley**, to garnish

Cook the rice in a saucepan of lightly salted water for 15 minutes, until tender, then drain.

Meanwhile, heat the oil in a large, heavy skillet, add the chorizo, onion, and chicken, and cook over medium heat, for 10 minutes, stirring occasionally, until browned and cooked through. Add the bell peppers and celery and cook, for another 5 minutes, stirring occasionally.

Blend the measured water with the cornstarch, then stir into the broth, add to the pan with the tomatoes, and bring to a boil. Reduce the heat and simmer for 5 minutes before adding the cooked rice. Season generously with black pepper.

Serve garnished with the parsley, accompanied by crusty bread and salad, if desired.

For Creole-style jambalaya, heat 1 tablespoon olive oil in a large saucepan, add 1 chopped onion, and cook over medium heat for 5 minutes, stirring occasionally. Add 8 oz sliced chorizo sausage, 4 chunkily shredded cooked chicken breasts, and 1 teaspoon Creole spice mix. Cook for 1 minute, then add 1½ cups tomato sauce, ½ cup chicken broth, and 3 cups cooked egg-fried rice. Stir, heat through, season, and serve. Total cooking time 10 minutes.

herb-stuffed chicken breasts

Serves **4**
Total cooking time **30 minutes**

4 **boneless, skinless chicken
  breasts**
⅔ cup **cream cheese**
2 **garlic cloves**, crushed
1½ teaspoons chopped
  parsley
1½ teaspoons chopped
  chives
10 slices of **prosciutto**
1½ teaspoons **vegetable oil**,
  for oiling
2 **leeks**, finely sliced
1¼ cups **fromage blanc**
  or **Greek yogurt**
salt and **black pepper**
crisp green salad, to serve

Using a sharp knife, make a slit in the side of each chicken breast to make a little pocket.

Mix together the cream cheese, garlic, herbs, and some salt and black pepper in a bowl.

Lay 2 slices of the prosciutto on a cutting board and place 1 of the chicken breasts on top. Spoon one-quarter of the cream cheese mixture into the chicken breast, then wrap around the prosciutto to seal the pocket. Repeat with the remaining prosciutto, cream cheese, and chicken to make 4 packages. Put into a roasting pan and bake in a preheated oven, at 400°F, for 20 minutes or until cooked through.

Meanwhile, chop the remaining prosciutto and cook in a lightly oiled skillet over medium heat for 1–2 minutes. Add the leeks and stir-fry for 2–3 minutes, then stir in the fromage blanc or Greek yogurt and some salt and black pepper.

Serve the chicken with a crisp green salad and the bacon and leek sauce.

For herb chicken pita pockets, mix ⅔ cup cream cheese with 2 tablespoons chopped fresh herbs of your choice. Toast 4 pita breads for 2–3 minutes on each side, then cut along the long side to open like a pocket. Spread the inside of each pita bread with the cream cheese. Slice 3 cooked chicken breasts, then stuff each pita bread with one-quarter of the chicken, 1 cup crisp salad greens, and a dollop of mango sauce. **Total cooking time 10 minutes.**

chicken & ham cobbler

Serves **4**

Total cooking time **30 minutes**

2 tablespoons **butter**

2 **leeks**, sliced

12 oz **boneless, skinless chicken thighs**, diced

5 oz **cured ham**, cut into small chunks

⅔ cup hot **chicken broth**

½ cup **crème fraîche** or **heavy cream**

1¼ cups **all-purpose flour**

1 tablespoon **baking powder**

2 tablespoons **olive oil**

⅔ cup **milk**

2 tablespoons **mixed herbs**, such as parsley, thyme, and chives, finely chopped

¼ cup shredded **cheddar cheese**

salt and **black pepper**

Melt the butter in a shallow, flameproof casserole dish, add the leeks, and cook for 3 minutes, until softened. Add the chicken and cook for 2 minutes, until lightly browned all over. Stir in the ham, broth, and crème fraîche or heavy cream, then season.

Mix the flour and baking powder in a bowl, then pour in the oil and milk. Mix gently, season well, and stir in the herbs and cheese.

Arrange spoonfuls of the dough on top of the chicken mixture, leaving a little space between each spoonful. Place in a preheated oven, at 425°F, for 15–20 minutes, until the topping is lightly browned and the chicken is cooked through.

For creamy chicken & ham pasta, cook 1 lb quick-cooking spaghetti in a large saucepan of lightly salted boiling water according to the package directions, adding 1 finely sliced leek for the last 5 minutes of cooking. Drain and return the pasta and leek to the pan. Stir in 2 shredded cooked chicken breasts and 4 slices of ham, torn into strips. Season well, add ¼ cup crème fraîche or heavy cream, then sprinkle with chopped parsley to serve. **Total cooking time 10 minutes.**

cajun chicken quinoa with apricots

Serves **4**

Total cooking time **30 minutes**

2½ cups **chicken broth**

½ cup **quinoa**

¾ cup coarsely chopped **dried apricots**

3 **skinless chicken breasts**, thinly sliced

2 teaspoons **Cajun spice mix**

2 tablespoons **olive oil**

2 **red onions**, cut into slim wedges

2 bunches of **scallions**, coarsely chopped

⅓ cup chopped **fresh cilantro**

Greek yogurt, to serve

Put the broth into a saucepan and bring to a boil, add the quinoa, then simmer for 10 minutes. Stir in the apricots and cook for another 5 minutes.

Meanwhile, toss the chicken with the Cajun spice in a bowl to coat. Heat the oil in a large, heavy skillet, add the chicken and onion wedges, and cook over medium-high heat for 10 minutes, stirring frequently, until the chicken is well browned and cooked through. Add the scallions and cook for another 1 minute.

Drain the quinoa and apricots, then add to the chicken mixture and toss well to mix. Toss in the chopped cilantro and serve with spoonfuls of Greek yogurt, with crusty bread, if desired.

For chicken with fresh apricot lentils, heat 1 tablespoon olive oil in a large skillet and cook 1 finely chopped red onion over medium heat for 5 minutes, stirring frequently. Pour in ¼ cup red wine vinegar and cook for 30 seconds. Add 1¼ cups cooked green lentils, 4 fresh pitted apricots cut into chunks, and ¼ cup each of chopped fresh cilantro and mint. Add 4 cups shredded cooked chicken breasts and heat through for 1 minute. To serve, stir in 2 cups arugula. **Total cooking time 10 minutes.**

thai meatballs with noodles

Serves **4**
Total cooking time **20 minutes**

1 lb **ground chicken**
3 **scallions,** finely diced
2 **garlic cloves,** finely diced
1 **red chile,** seeded and finely
   diced
2 inch piece of **fresh ginger
   root,** peeled and finely diced
2½ cups **chicken broth**
1 lb **rice noodles**
1¼ cups **prepared tomato
   sauce,** heated
fresh cilantro leaves,
   to garnish

Mix together the ground chicken, scallions, garlic, chile, and ginger. Using wet hands, divide the chicken mixture into 16 portions and roll into balls.

Pour the broth into a large saucepan and bring to a boil. Add the meatballs and simmer for 10 minutes.

Meanwhile, cook the rice noodles according to the package directions, then drain and serve them topped with the meatballs and tomato sauce, garnished with cilantro leaves.

For Thai chicken curry with noodles, heat 1 tablespoon vegetable oil in a wok over high heat, add 2 diced shallots and 1 diced lemon grass stick, and cook for 1–2 minutes. Stir in 3–4 teaspoons red Thai curry paste and cook for 1 minute, stirring. Add 1¼ lb boneless, skinless chicken breasts, cut into bite-size pieces, and stir-fry for 5–6 minutes. Add 1½ teaspoons Thai fish sauce, 1 teaspoon packed brown sugar, and a couple of lime leaves with 1¾ cups coconut milk. Bring to a simmer and cook for 15 minutes, until the chicken is cooked through. Cook 8 oz rice noodles according to the package directions. Stir a small handful of coarsely torn cilantro leaves into the curry and serve with the rice noodles. **Total cooking time 30 minutes.**

food for
friends

chicken & goat cheese tarts

Serves **4**

Total cooking time **30 minutes**

1 sheet **ready-to-bake
   puff pastry**, cut into
   4 equal rectangles
2 tablespoons **olive oil**
8 oz **boneless, skinless
   chicken breasts**, diced
7 cups **fresh spinach**
½ teaspoon **ground nutmeg**
1 teaspoon **mustard seeds**
½ cup **prepared onion relish**
8 thick slices of **rindless
   goat cheese**
salt and **black pepper**

Put the 4 pastry rectangles onto a large baking sheet and prick all over with a fork.

Heat the oil in a large, heavy skillet and cook the chicken over high heat for 3 minutes. Add the spinach, toss, and cook for 1 minute, until wilted. Remove from the heat, add the nutmeg and mustard seeds, and season with a little salt and black pepper, tossing well to coat.

Drain the mixture, if necessary, then spoon evenly onto the 4 pastry rectangles to within 1 inch of the edges. Spoon 2 tablespoons of onion relish over the top of each and put the goat cheese on top. Bake in a preheated oven, at 425°F, for 20 minutes, until puffed and golden. Serve with a salad.

For chicken, spinach & goat cheese tarts, heat 1 tablespoon olive oil and 1 tablespoon butter in a large, heavy skillet and cook 8 oz diced boneless, skinless chicken breasts for 5 minutes. Add 3½ cups spinach and toss and stir for 2 minutes. Add ½ teaspoon ground nutmeg and season well. Chop 2 oz rindless goat cheese into small cubes and stir into the chicken and spinach. Spoon the mixture into 4 prepared pastry shells and serve with salad. **Total cooking time 10 minutes.**

sesame chicken & noodles

Serves **4**
Total cooking time **20 minutes**

12 oz **boneless, skinless chicken breasts** or **thighs**, cut into thin strips
2 teaspoons **cornstarch**
1 tablespoon **dark soy sauce**
1 ½ tablespoons **sesame oil**
2 teaspoons **sesame seeds**, plus extra to serve
2 teaspoons **honey**
2 tablespoons **vegetable oil**
1 **onion**, thinly sliced
1 **red bell pepper**, cored, seeded, and thinly sliced
1 medium-large **zucchini**, thinly sliced
1 tablespoon peeled and finely chopped **fresh ginger root** (optional)
1 lb **dried medium egg noodles**
½ cup **water**

Mix the chicken with the cornstarch, soy sauce, 1 tablespoon of the sesame oil, the sesame seeds, and honey. Let marinate.

Heat the vegetable oil in a large skillet or wok, add the onion and red bell pepper, and cook for 3–4 minutes, until slightly softened. Add the zucchini and ginger, if using, and cook for another 4–5 minutes, stirring frequently, until slightly softened.

Meanwhile, bring a large saucepan of water to a boil, add the egg noodles, and immediately remove from the heat. Cover and set aside for 4–5 minutes, until tender. Alternatively, cook according to the package directions. Drain and refresh under cold running water, then toss in the remaining sesame oil.

Add the chicken and its marinade to the vegetables and cook gently for 1–2 minutes to seal. Stir in the measured water and simmer for 2–3 minutes, until the chicken is cooked through and the sauce thickened.

Stir the noodles into the pan and cook for 1–2 minutes, until hot, then pile into bowls and serve sprinkled with extra sesame seeds.

For sesame chicken noodle salad, cook and cool 1 lb dried medium egg noodles, as above. Toss with 1 sliced red bel pepper, 2 sliced scallions, 1 ½ cups bean sprouts, and 2 cups cooked chicken strips. Mix together 2 tablespoons vegetable oil, 1 ½ tablespoons sesame oil, 2 teaspoons honey, 1 tablespoon dark soy sauce, and 1 teaspoon finely grated fresh ginger root, then toss into the noodles. Sprinkle with sesame seeds. **Total cooking time 10 minutes.**

cacciatore-style chicken pasta

Serves **4**

Total cooking time **20 minutes**

3 tablespoons **olive oil**

1 **red onion**, thinly sliced

2 **garlic cloves**, chopped

2 **large boneless, skinless chicken breasts** (about 6 oz each), thinly sliced

4 oz **salami**, thinly sliced and halved

½ cup **red wine**

2 **rosemary sprigs**, leaves chopped

2 (14½ oz) cans **cherry tomatoes**

¾ cup pitted **green olives** (optional)

1 lb **short pasta shapes**, such as fusilli

salt and **black pepper**

Heat the oil in a large skillet and cook the onion and garlic over medium-high heat for 4–5 minutes, until slightly softened. Add the chicken and salami and cook for another 3–4 minutes, until lightly golden.

Pour the wine into the pan and simmer until completely evaporated. Add the rosemary, tomatoes, and olives, if using, and simmer for 8–10 minutes, until thickened slightly. Season with salt and black pepper.

Meanwhile, cook the pasta in a large saucepan of lightly salted boiling water for about 11 minutes, or according to the package directions, until "al dente." Drain and pile into 4 serving bowls. Top with the sauce and serve.

For cacciatore chicken & salami ciabatta, heat 2 tablespoons olive oil in a skillet and cook 12 oz chicken strips over medium-high heat for 8 minutes, turning occasionally, or until cooked through and golden brown. Transfer to a plate and set aside. Meanwhile, cut 1 large ciabatta loaf into 8 sandwich slices. Divide 4 oz sliced salami among 4 pieces of the bread. Slice 8 cherry tomatoes, ½ cup pitted green olives, and ½ small red onion. Put a little of each on top of the salami, then add some of the chicken and a small handful of arugula. Cover with the remaining bread and serve. **Total cooking time 10 minutes.**

chicken fettuccine alfredo

Serves **4**
Total cooking time **20 minutes**

2 **boneless, skinless
    chicken breasts**
1 lb **fettuccine**
2 tablespoons **butter**
½ cup **light cream**
½ cup grated **Parmesan
    cheese**
salt and **black pepper**
finely sliced **chives**, to garnish

Put the chicken breasts into a small saucepan, pour over enough water to cover, and simmer for 12–15 minutes or until just cooked through.

Meanwhile, cook the pasta in a large saucepan of salted boiling water according to the package directions until "al dente."

Melt the butter in a separate saucepan, stir in the cream, and simmer for 1–2 minutes, then season well. Using a fork, break the chicken into bite-size pieces.

Drain the pasta, reserving a little of the cooking water, and return to the pan. Toss through the chicken, creamy sauce, and Parmesan, adding a little cooking water to loosen, if needed. Season well.

Spoon into 4 serving bowls and serve sprinkled with the chives.

For quick chicken spaghetti alfredo, cook 1 lb quick-cooking spaghetti and the cream sauce as above. Drain the pasta, reserving a little of the cooking water, and return to the pan. Toss through 2 cooked roasted chicken breasts, skin discarded and torn into shreds, the sauce, and Parmesan as above. Serve immediately. **Total cooking time 10 minutes.**

chicken & olive couscous

Serves **4**

Total cooking time **10 minutes**

¼ cup **olive oil**

½ **lemon** (zest and flesh),
  finely chopped

1 tablespoon **honey**

½ teaspoon **ground cumin**

1 **garlic clove**, crushed

1½ cups **couscous**

1¼ cups hot **chicken broth**

1 (15 oz) can **chickpeas
  (garbanzo beans)**, rinsed
  and drained

½ cup pitted **green olives**

2 **cooked chicken breasts**,
  sliced

handful each of **fresh cilantro**
  and **mint**, chopped

salt and **black pepper**

Heat the oil and lemon in a saucepan and cook over gentle heat for about 2 minutes, until the lemon is soft.

Stir in the honey, cumin, and garlic and heat through. Stir in the couscous, broth, chickpeas (garbanzo beans), olives, and chicken.

Remove from the heat, cover, and let stand for 5 minutes, until the couscous is tender. Fluff up with a fork and stir in the cilantro and mint. Season and serve immediately.

For cumin-dusted chicken breasts with spicy olive couscous, heat 2 tablespoons olive oil in a skillet. Dust 4 small boneless, skinless chicken breasts with 1 teaspoon ground cumin, season, and cook for 5 minutes on each side, until just cooked through. Stir in 1 crushed garlic clove and 2 teaspoons harissa or chili paste. Add 1½ cups couscous, 1¼ cups hot chicken broth, and ½ cup green olives. Cover and let stand for 5 minutes, until the couscous is tender. Fluff up with a fork and stir in a handful each of chopped mint and fresh cilantro and the grated zest and juice of ½ lemon. **Total cooking time 20 minutes.**

quick coq au vin

Serves **4**

Total cooking time **30 minutes**

2 tablespoons **olive oil**

8 **chicken drumsticks**

8 **bacon slices**, coarsely
chopped

8 **whole shallots**

8 oz **cremini mushrooms**,
halved

1 tablespoon **all-purpose
flour**

2 tablespoons **thyme leaves**

1 ¼ cups **red wine**

2 cups **rich chicken broth**

thyme sprigs, to garnish

mashed potatoes, to serve

Heat the oil in a large, heavy skillet, add the drumsticks
and bacon, and cook over high heat for 5 minutes.
Add the shallots and mushrooms and cook for another
5 minutes, turning the chicken and shallots, until golden
brown all over. Add the flour and toss to coat, then add
the thyme.

Pour in the wine and broth and bring to a boil, stirring
continually to distribute the flour evenly within the sauce.
Reduce the heat and simmer, uncovered, for 15 minutes,
until the chicken is cooked through.

Garnish the coq au vin with thyme sprigs and
serve ladled onto hot mashed potatoes in 4 warm
serving bowls.

For chicken, mushroom & red wine soup with
croutons, heat 1 tablespoon olive oil in a saucepan and
cook 1 diced large boneless, skinless chicken breast
with 1 chopped onion and 2 cups coarsely chopped
white button mushrooms over high heat for 5 minutes
until the chicken is cooked through. Meanwhile, make
1 (2 oz) envelope red wine sauce mix according to
the package directions and add to the chicken with
1 ¼ cups chicken broth. Bring to a boil, ladle into warm
serving bowls, and serve sprinkled with prepared
croutons. **Total cooking time 10 minutes.**

chicken & brie puff pie

Serves **4**

Total cooking time **20 minutes**

1 sheet **ready-to-bake
   puff pastry**

1 medium **egg**, beaten

1 tablespoon **olive oil**

2 **leeks**, chopped

2 cups halved **baby white
   button mushrooms**

2½ cups diced **cooked
   chicken**

4 oz **Brie cheese**, sliced

4 slices of **prosciutto**,
   cut into strips

1 teaspoon chopped **thyme
   leaves** (optional)

¼ cup **low-fat crème fraîche**
   or **heavy cream**

salt and **black pepper**

Line a baking sheet with parchment paper. Unroll the pastry, place a pie dish on it upside down, and cut around it. Put the pastry onto the prepared sheet, brush with beaten egg, and bake in a preheated oven, at 400°F, for about 10 minutes, until puffed up and pale golden.

Meanwhile, heat the oil in a large skillet, add the leeks, and cook for 3–4 minutes, until softened. Add the mushrooms and cook for another 3–4 minutes, until soft and golden. Add the remaining ingredients, season, and cook until the chicken is hot.

Put the filling into the pie dish, top with the pastry lid, and return to the oven for 3–4 minutes or until the pastry is golden and crisp.

For chicken, Brie & thyme melts, slice 1 baguette in half lengthwise and then widthwise to make 4 equal pieces. Spread each cut side with 2 tablespoons onion relish. Divide 1⅓ cups chunky sliced cooked chicken, 4 oz sliced Brie, 8 halved cherry tomatoes, and 1 teaspoon thyme leaves among each on the bread. Drizzle each slice with ½ teaspoon olive oil, put onto a rack, and slide under a preheated medium-hot broiler for 5–6 minutes, until melted and golden. Serve with arugula. **Total cooking time 10 minutes.**

feta-stuffed chicken with peppers

Serves **4**
Total cooking time **30 minutes**

1 (6 oz) package **feta cheese,**
  crumbled (about 1 cup)
1 **red chile,** seeded and
  chopped
2 teaspoons rinsed **capers**
1 teaspoon grated **lemon** zest
¾ cup **pitted olives,** sliced
2 tablespoons chopped **fresh
  cilantro** or **parsley**
2 tablespoons **olive oil**
4 **boneless chicken breasts,**
  skin on
4 **lemon** wedges
2 **Romano peppers,** halved
  lengthwise and seeded
1½ cups **couscous**
salt and **black pepper**

Put the feta into a small bowl and add the chile, capers, lemon zest, olives, cilantro or parsley, and half the olive oil. Season generously with salt and black pepper.

Cut a pocket in the side of each chicken breast and fill with half the feta mixture. Place, skin side up, in an ovenproof dish with the lemon wedges and Romano peppers.

Drizzle with the remaining olive oil and place in a preheated oven, at 425°F, for about 20 minutes, until the chicken is cooked and golden brown.

Meanwhile, cook the couscous according to the package directions, fluff up with a fork, and fold in the remaining feta mixture. Spoon onto plates and serve with the stuffed chicken, roasted peppers, and lemon wedges.

For spicy chicken & feta rolls, put 2 cups sliced cooked chicken breasts into a large bowl with the feta, chile, capers, olives, and cilantro from the main recipe. Add 1 tablespoon olive oil, 2 teaspoons lemon juice, 3 cups arugula, and a pinch of salt and black pepper. Toss to combine, then pile onto 4 large, soft flour tortillas. Roll up the tortillas and toast them on a hot ridged grill pan for 4–5 minutes, turning occasionally, until warm and charred. Cut in half diagonally and serve with a tabbouleh salad or steamed couscous for a more substantial meal. **Total cooking time 10 minutes.**

chicken parmigiana with fusilli

Serves **4**

Total cooking time **20 minutes**

2 cups **fresh white bread crumbs**

¼ cup grated **Parmesan cheese**

¼ cup **olive oil**, plus extra for greasing

4 small **boneless, skinless chicken breasts**

4 oz **mozzarella cheese**, cut into 4 slices

12 oz **fusilli lunghi**

1 cup **prepared tomato sauce**

salt and **black pepper**

green salad, to serve

Mix together the bread crumbs and Parmesan on a large plate and season. Rub about 2 teaspoons of the oil over each chicken breast, press down with your palm to flatten a little, then dip in the bread crumb mixture until coated all over. Put the chicken breats onto a lightly greased broiler pan.

Drizzle with a little more oil, then cook under a preheated hot broiler for 10 minutes, turning once, until golden brown and cooked through. Top each chicken breast with a slice of mozzarella and cook for another 2 minutes or until the cheese has melted.

Meanwhile, cook the pasta in a large saucepan of salted boiling water according to the package directions until "al dente." Heat the tomato sauce in a small saucepan. Drain the pasta and toss through the sauce. Cut each chicken breast in half. Spoon into serving bowls and top with the broiled chicken. Serve with green salad.

For easy chicken, mozzarella & tomato spaghetti,

heat 1 tablespoon olive oil in a wok or large skillet, add 12 oz chicken strips, and stir-fry for 7 minutes or until just cooked through. Pour over 1 cup store-bought tomato sauce and simmer for 1–2 minutes. Meanwhile, cook 1 lb spaghetti according to the package directions until "al dente." Drain and return to the pan. Cut 4 oz mozzarella cheese into small chunks and stir through the pasta with the chicken sauce. Serve immediately. **Total cooking time 10 minutes.**

baked chicken with gremolata

Serves **4**

Total cooking time **20 minutes**

1 lb **new potatoes**, thinly
   sliced

3 tablespoons **olive oil**

4 **boneless, skinless chicken
   breasts** (about 5 oz each)

4 oz **asparagus**, trimmed

salt and **black pepper**

Gremolata

1 **garlic clove**, finely chopped

finely grated zest of 1 **lemon**

large handful of chopped
   parsley

Toss the potatoes with 2 tablespoons of the oil and put into a large, shallow roasting pan. Place in a preheated oven, at 400°F, for 5 minutes, then arrange the chicken breasts on top and drizzle with a little more oil. Season well and return to the oven for another 10 minutes.

Arrange the asparagus spears in the pan, pour any remaining oil over them, and return to the oven for another 5 minutes, until the chicken and potatoes are golden and cooked through.

Meanwhile, make the gremolata. Mix together the garlic, lemon zest, and parsley. Sprinkle it over the chicken and vegetables before serving.

For chicken, asparagus & gremolata frittata, heat 2 tablespoons olive oil in a large, nonstick skillet. Add 4 oz asparagus tips and 1 crushed garlic clove and cook for 5 minutes, until tender. Mix 1 cooked chicken breast, cut into bite-size pieces, with 6 beaten eggs, the finely grated zest of 1 lemon, and a handful of chopped parsley. Season and pour into the pan, mix gently together, then cook over low heat for 15 minutes or until the egg is cooked through. **Total cooking time 30 minutes.**

chicken with mustard sauce

Serves **4**

Total cooking time **25 minutes**

1 tablespoon **olive oil**

1 tablespoon **butter**

4 **boneless, skinless chicken breasts** (about 5 oz each)

1 cup **crème fraîche** or **heavy cream**

1 tablespoon **whole-grain mustard**

1 teaspoon **English mustard**

1 teaspoon **Dijon mustard**

3 tablespoons chopped **parsley**

black pepper

To serve

green beans

new potatoes

Heat the oil and butter in a large, heavy skillet and cook the chicken over high heat for 20 minutes, turning once, or until golden and cooked through. Use a spatula to remove the chicken from the pan and keep it warm.

Add the crème fraîche or heavy cream to the pan with the mustards and stir for 2–3 minutes, until warm but not boiled. Stir in the chopped parsley and season generously with black pepper. Divide the chicken among warm serving plates and spoon the sauce over them. Serve with green beans and buttered new potatoes.

For creamy chicken pan-fry with hot mustard sauce, heat 2 tablespoons butter in a saucepan and cook 2 diced large boneless, skinless chicken breasts (about 6 oz each) over high heat for 7–8 minutes or until golden brown and cooked through. Add 1 tablespoon Dijon mustard, 2 teaspoons English mustard, and 1 teaspoon whole-grain mustard. Stir well, then add ⅔ cup heavy cream. Stir and heat for 2 minutes, until piping hot. Spoon onto warm serving plates and garnish with parsley sprigs. **Total cooking time 10 minutes.**

roasted chicken & vegetables

Serves **4**
Total cooking time **30 minutes**

¼ cup **olive oil**
4 **boneless chicken breasts**,
  skin on
1 lb small **waxy potatoes**,
  halved
6 **carrots**, quartered
3 **parsnips**, cored and
  quartered
4 **banana shallots**, quartered
6 small **garlic cloves**
2 **thyme sprigs**
rosemary sprig
salt and **black pepper**

Heat half the oil in a large skillet over medium-high heat, add the chicken, skin side down, and cook without moving for 7–8 minutes, until the skin is really crisp and golden brown.

Meanwhile, parboil the potatoes in a large saucepan of salted boiling water for 6–7 minutes, adding the carrots and parsnips for the final 3 minutes. They should all be starting to soften.

Drain well and put into a large roasting pan. Add the shallots, garlic, herbs, and remaining oil, season generously, and toss well. Nestle the chicken in with the vegetables, skin side up.

Roast in a preheated oven, at 425°F, for 20 minutes, until the chicken is cooked through and the vegetables are golden brown. Serve with steamed kale, if desired.

For pan-fried chicken with roasted vegetables, add 1 (16 oz) bag mixed vegetable, such as carrots and broccoli, to a large roasting pan with 1 lb halved baby new potatoes. Toss with 3 tablespoons olive oil, 2 thyme sprigs, and a generous pinch of salt and black pepper. Roast in a preheated oven, at 450°F, for 18 minutes, shaking the pan occasionally, until tender and golden. Meanwhile, heat 2 tablespoons olive oil in a large skillet and cook 4 seasoned boneless chicken breasts, skin side down, for 8–10 minutes, until golden brown. Turn the chicken and cook for another 3–5 minutes or until the juices run clear. Serve the chicken with the roasted vegetables. **Total cooking time 20 minutes.**

chicken & mushroom rice

Serves **4**
Total cooking time **10 minutes**

4 tablespoons **butter**
3 **scallions**, sliced
2 **cooked roasted chicken
breasts**, sliced or shredded
1 (1 lb) package **long-grain
and wild rice mixture**,
cooked according to
package directions
1 (9 oz) **jar mushroom
antipasti**, drained
¼ cup **crème fraîche** or
Greek yogurt
salt and **black pepper**

Melt the butter in a large skillet, add the scallions, and cook over medium heat for 2–3 minutes, until softened. Add the chicken, rice, and all but a small handful of the mushrooms. Stir-fry for 3–4 minutes, until piping hot.

Add the crème fraîche or yogurt, season, and stir occasionally for about 2 minutes, until hot and creamy. Spoon into shallow bowls and serve immediately, topped with the reserved mushrooms.

For chicken & mushroom fried rice, cook 2 cups quick-cooking long-grain rice for 8–9 minutes, or according to the package directions, until just tender. Drain well. Heat 2 tablespoons vegetable oil in a large skillet or wok, add 3 sliced scallions and 2 chopped garlic cloves, and sauté for 2–3 minutes. Add 3 cups diced cremini mushrooms and the shredded chicken from the main recipe and stir-fry for 3–4 minutes, until soft and golden brown. Increase the heat slightly and add the rice and ½ cup defrosted peas. Stir-fry for 3–4 minutes, until hot and lightly golden. Season, then spoon into bowls and serve with soy sauce. **Total cooking time 20 minutes.**

linguine with marsala chicken

Serves **4**
Total cooking time **30 minutes**

3 tablespoons **olive oil**
2 **boneless chicken breasts**
1 **shallot**, finely sliced
²⁄₃ cup **Marsala** or **sherry**
²⁄₃ cup hot **chicken broth**
1 **sage leaf**, finely chopped
½ cup **heavy cream**
8 oz **cremini mushrooms**,
   halved if large
1 lb **linguine**
salt and **black pepper**
chopped **flat leaf parsley**,
   to garnish

Heat 1 tablespoon of the oil in a skillet. Season the chicken breasts well, add them to the pan, and cook for 5–7 minutes on each side or until golden brown and cooked through.

Meanwhile, heat 1 tablespoon of the oil in a saucepan, add the shallot, and cook over low heat for a couple of minutes, until softened. Pour in the Marsala or sherry, increase the heat to high, and cook for a couple of minutes, until reduced and slightly syrupy. Add the broth and sage and simmer for another 5 minutes. Stir in the cream, season well, and keep warm.

Cut the chicken into slices and add to the sauce. Add the remaining oil to the skillet and cook the mushrooms for 3–5 minutes, until golden brown all over, then stir into the sauce.

Meanwhile, cook the pasta in a large saucepan of salted boiling water according to the package directions. Drain, reserving a little of the cooking water, and return to the pan. Toss through the sauce, adding cooking water to loosen, if needed. Season and sprinkle with parsley.

For linguine with poached chicken in Marsala, put 2 boneless, skinless chicken breasts into a saucepan and pour ½ cup Marsala or sherry over them along with enough chicken broth to cover and poach gently for 15 minutes or until cooked through. Meanwhile, cook and drain the linguine and sauté the mushrooms as above. Cut the chicken into strips and stir through the drained pasta with the mushrooms, a little of the poaching liquid (boiled down, if desired) to loosen, and some heavy cream. Serve immediately. **Total cooking time 20 minutes.**

index

apricots
Cajun chicken quinoa with apricots 200
chicken & apricot couscous 116
chicken & apricot Moroccan couscous 56
chicken & apricot stew 82
chicken & apricot wraps 82
chicken with fresh apricot lentils 200
herb quinoa & chicken 56
Moroccan fruity chicken stew 98
spicy chicken & fruit couscous salad 116

asparagus
baked chicken with gremolata 224
chicken & asparagus calzone 44
chicken, asparagus & gremolata frittata 224
smoked chicken, asparagus & blue cheese salad 44

avocados
Cajun chicken & avocado melt 14
chicken, avocado & mustard sandwiches 156
chicken kebabs with avocado dip 62
curried chicken with avocado 62

bacon
bacon & chicken pasta 184
chicken & ham sandwiches 24
chicken, bacon & zucchini baguettes 38
chicken club sandwich 26
citrus baked chicken 66
creamy chicken rice 176
creamy cider chicken 176
quick coq au vin 216

bagels
creamy chicken on bagels 12

baguettes
chicken, bacon & zucchini baguettes 38
chicken, brie & thyme melts 218
chicken Caesar baguettes 48
chicken, lemon & tarragon baguettes 148
chicken pesto baguettes 60

balsamic vinegar
balsamic chicken bruschetta 178
balsamic chicken wraps 20
sweet balsamic chicken 178

bell peppers
chicken & couscous stuffed bell peppers 54
ginger chicken wraps 30
piquant chicken & mixed pepper salad 124

bok choy
chicken & Asian vegetable stir-fry 96
saucy lemon chicken with greens 80

brie
chicken & brie puff pie 218
chicken, brie & thyme melts 218

brochettes
piquant chicken brochettes 124

bruschetta
balsamic chicken bruschetta 178

burgers see also patties
chicken & tarragon burgers 164
crunchy chicken burgers with tarragon mayonnaise 164
Mexican chicken burgers 158
Thai-style chicken patties 120
Thai chicken burgers 144

cabbage, red
coleslaw 84

calzone
chicken & asparagus calzone 44

cauliflower
chicken pilaf with cauliflower 94

chapatis
spicy chicken & mango chutney chapati wraps 22

cheddar cheese
Cajun chicken hot open sandwich 14
loaded chicken nachos 158
chicken & apple soup 28

chicken livers
chicken liver & mustard pâté 64
chicken liver salad 64

chickpeas (garbanzo beans)
chicken & apricot Moroccan couscous 56
chicken & olive couscous 214
chicken couscous salad 54
harissa chicken 134
hummus 70
Moroccan chicken & bean soup 98
Moroccan fruity chicken stew 98

chiles
baked spicy chicken 162
chicken salad with spicy arugula pesto 140
chicken with spicy arugula pesto 140
feta-stuffed chicken with peppers 220
hot & sour chicken salad 34
pasta with chili chicken sauce 162
spicy chicken & feta rolls 220
spicy chicken & rosemary creamy pasta 112

spicy chicken &
rosemary soup 112
spicy chicken nachos
18
chorizo
chicken & mozzarella
packages 102
Creole-style jambalaya
194
ciabatta loaf
cacciatore chicken
& salami ciabatta
210
Cajun chicken &
avocado melt 14
chicken Caesar salad
32
chicken Caesar with
garlicky croutons
32
yogurt chicken &
spinach ciabatta
58
cider
creamy cider chicken
176
cobbler
chicken & ham
cobbler 198
coleslaw 84
coq-au-vin, quick 216
crepes
curried chicken with
avocado 62
spicy chicken crepes
126
couscous
chicken & apricot
couscous 116
chicken & apricot
Moroccan couscous
56
chicken & couscous
stuffed bell peppers
54
chicken & olive
couscous 214

chicken couscous
salad 54
cumin-dusted chicken
breasts with olive
couscous 214
harissa chicken 134
spicy chicken & fruit
couscous salad 116
cream cheese
crispy stuffed chicken
breasts 104
cucumber
Chinese chicken
wraps 76
tandoori chicken
wings with raita 36
curries
broiled chicken with
curry mayonnaise
114
broiled korma chicken
with rice 92
chicken biryani 146
curried chicken &
grape salad 114
curried chicken &
peas 136
curried chicken & rice
122
curried chicken with
vegetable rice 94
mild & creamy chicken
curry 92
quick chicken & pea
curry 136
quick Thai green
chicken curry 152
simple fruity chicken
biryani 146
Thai chicken curry
with noodles
202
Thai red curry with
chicken balls 144
cutlets
Parmesan chicken
cutlets 48

dips
avocado 62
chile & red onion 118
dressings
honey & mustard 84,
156
lemon mint 40
olive oil & lemon 58
olive oil & mint 72
pesto 60, 102
spicy yogurt 126
drumsticks
sticky soy-glazed
drumsticks 190

eggplants
chicken & eggplant
casserole 86
chicken, eggplant
& tomato soup 86
quick chicken
moussaka 106
eggs see frittatas;
omelets

fennel
fennel, chicken
& tomato pasta 42
fennel, chicken &
tomato pizza 42
feta cheese
feta-stuffed chicken
with peppers
220
spicy chicken & feta
rolls 220
yogurt chicken with
greek salad 58
Fontina cheese
stuffed chicken
breasts 24
frittatas
chicken & cheese
frittata 50
chicken, asparagus
& gremolata frittata
224

garbanzo beans see
chickpeas
garlic baked mushrooms
with
chicken 12
ginger chicken soup
30
ginger chicken wraps
30
goat cheese
chicken & goat
cheese panini 16
chicken & goat
cheese pizza 16
chicken & goat
cheese tarts 206
chicken, spinach &
goat cheese tarts
206
gremolata
baked chicken with
gremolata 224
chicken, asparagus
& gremolata frittata
224
Gruyère cheese
cheesy chicken
omelet 50
chicken & cheese
frittata 50

ham
chicken & ham
cobbler 198
chicken, ham &
cheese packages
184
creamy chicken &
ham pasta 198
herb-stuffed chicken
breasts 196
stuffed chicken
breasts 24
harissa
harissa chicken 134
yogurt & harissa
chicken kebabs 134

hummus
  chicken dippers with
    hummus 70
  hot chicken &
    hummus pita
      pockets 46
  spiced chicken
    breasts with
      hummus 70

jambalaya 194

kebabs see also
    skewers
  chicken & mango
    kebabs 180
  chicken kebabs
    with avocado dip
      62
  chicken & zucchini
    kebabs 38
  nectarine-glazed
    chicken kebabs 72
  yogurt & harissa
    chicken kebabs 134
kidney beans
  Tex–Mex chicken &
    beans 68
koftas, chicken 106

lemons
  chicken, lemon &
    tarragon baguettes
      148
  crunchy lemon
    chicken salad 192
  lemon & parsley
    chicken skewers
      170
  lemon & parsley-
    stuffed chicken 170
  lemon chicken pita
    pockets 40
  lemon, mint & chicken
    skewers 40
  lemon noodle chicken
    80

roasted lemon chicken
  with broccoli 188
saucy lemon chicken
  with greens 80
spicy lemon chicken
  salad 130
sticky lemon chicken
  noodles 188
stir-fried lemon
  chicken 192
lentils, green
  chicken with fresh
    apricot lentils 200
limes
  baked chicken with
    lime 160
  chicken & lime noodle
    salad 160

mango chutney
  spicy chicken &
    mango chutney
      chapati wraps 22
mangos
  chicken & mango
    kebabs 180
  chicken & mango
    noodles 150
  mango & peanut
    chicken salad 180
  spicy chicken &
    mango skewers
      150
mayonnaise
  basil & lemon 174
  chicken with cilantro
    mayonnaise 78
  curry 114
  tarragon 164
meatballs
  Thai meatballs with
    noodles 202
  Thai red curry with
    chicken balls 144
moussaka, quick
  chicken 106
mozzarella cheese

bacon & chicken pasta
  184
Cajun chicken &
  avocado melt 14
chicken & eggplant
  casserole 86
chicken, ham &
  cheese packages
    184
chicken & mozzarella
  packages 102
chicken parmigiana
  with fusilli 222
easy chicken,
  mozzarella & tomato
    spaghetti 222
fennel, chicken &
  tomato pizza 42
spicy chicken naans
  22
mushrooms
  chicken & mushroom
    fried rice 230
  chicken & mushroom
    rice 230
  chicken, mushroom
    & red wine soup
      216
  creamy chicken on
    bagels 12
  garlic baked
    mushrooms with
      chicken 12
  hot & sour chicken
    salad 34
  hot & sour chicken
    soup 34
  linguine with Marsala
    chicken 232
  linguine with poached
    chicken in Marsala
      232
  quick coq au vin 216

naan bread
  spicy chicken naans
    22

tandoori chicken
  & salad naans 74
nachos
  spicy chicken nachos
    18
  loaded chicken
    nachos 158
nectarines
  chicken & nectarine
    salad 72
  nectarine-glazed
    chicken kebabs 72
noodles
  lemon noodle chicken
    80
  soy noodles with
    chicken 168
noodles, egg
  chicken & mango
    noodles 150
  chicken noodle broth
    110
  chicken noodle salad
    110
  ginger chicken soup
    30
  sesame chicken &
    noodles 208
  sesame chicken
    noodle salad 208
  sticky lemon chicken
    noodles 188
  sweet & spicy chicken
    noodles 132
noodles, rice
  chicken & lime noodle
    salad 160
  chicken noodle soup
    172
  chicken pad thai 172
  soy chicken & rice
    noodles 168
  Thai chicken curry
    with noodles
      202
  Thai meatballs with
    noodles 202

Thai-style chicken
patties 120

olives
chicken & olive
couscous 214
chicken, orange &
olive sandwiches 88
chicken with orange &
olives 88
cumin-dusted chicken
breasts with spicy
olive couscous 214
omelet, cheesy chicken
50
oranges
chicken, orange &
olive sandwiches 88
chicken with orange &
olives 88
citrus baked chicken
66
citrus chicken salad
66

Pad Thai
chicken Pad Thai 172
pancakes
teriyaki chicken rolls
100
panini, chicken & goat
cheese 16
Parmesan cheese
chicken parmigiana
with fusilli 222
Parmesan chicken
cutlets 48
pasta
cacciatore-style
chicken pasta
210
chicken & tarragon
pesto penne 182
chicken fettuccine
alfredo 212
chicken parmigiana
with fusilli 222

chicken pasta salad
with pesto 60
creamy chicken &
ham pasta 198
creamy chicken pasta
186
easy chicken,
mozzarella & tomato
spaghetti 222
fennel, chicken &
tomato pasta 42
linguine with Marsala
chicken 232
linguine with poached
chicken in Marsala
232
pasta with chili
chicken sauce 162
quick chicken
spaghetti alfredo
212
spicy chicken &
rosemary creamy
pasta 112
pastries see also pies;
tarts
chicken & shrimp
spring rolls 100
chicken phyllo pastries
with plum sauce
76
curried chicken
samosas 122
pâté, chicken liver &
mustard 64
patties see also burgers
Thai-style chicken
patties 120
peanut butter
chicken & vegetable
satay 166
mango & peanut
chicken salad
180
peanuts
chicken satay with
satay sauce 166

peas
curried chicken &
peas 136
quick chicken & pea
curry 136
sweet & spicy chicken
& pea rice 132
pesto
chicken & goat
cheese panini
16
chicken & tarragon
pesto penne
182
chicken & tomato
salad with pesto
dressing 102
chicken pasta salad
with pesto 60
chicken pesto
baguettes 60
chicken salad with
spicy arugula pesto
140
chicken with spicy
arugula pesto 140
pies see also pastries;
tarts
chicken & brie puff
pie 218
pilaf
chicken pilaf with
cauliflower 94
pita bread
chicken souvlaki
46
herb chicken pita
pockets 196
hot chicken &
hummus pita
pockets 46
lemon chicken pita
pockets 40
lemon, mint & chicken
skewers 40
tandoori chicken pita
pockets 36

pizzas
chicken & goat
cheese pizza 16
fennel, chicken &
tomato pizza 42

quesadillas, chicken 18
quinoa
Cajun chicken quinoa
with apricots 200
herb quinoa & chicken
56

raita
tandoori chicken
wings with raita 36
refried beans
chicken quesadillas
18
spicy chicken nachos
18
rice
baked chicken with
lime 160
chicken & mushroom
fried rice 230
chicken & mushroom
rice 230
chicken biryani 146
creamy chicken rice
176
curried chicken & rice
122
curried chicken with
vegetable rice
94
simple fruity chicken
biryani 146
sweet & spicy chicken
& pea rice 132
Vietnamese chicken,
herb & rice salad
128
Vietnamese herb
chicken rice 128
warm green chicken
& rice salad 118

risotto, spicy chicken 148
roasted chicken
  roasted chicken & vegetables 228
  roasted lemon chicken with broccoli 188
Roquefort cheese
  chicken & asparagus calzone 44

salads
  chicken & lime noodle salad 160
  chicken & nectarine salad 72
  chicken & tomato salad with pesto dressing 102
  chicken Caesar salad 32
  chicken Caesar with garlicky croutons 32
  chicken couscous salad 54
  chicken liver salad 64
  chicken, mushroom & spinach salad with spicy yogurt dressing 126
  chicken noodle salad 110
  chicken pasta salad with pesto 60
  chicken salad with spicy arugula pesto 140
  chicken salad wraps 26
  citrus chicken salad 66
  curried chicken with avocado 62
  crunchy lemon chicken salad 192
  curried chicken & grape salad 114
  honey & mustard chicken salad 156
  honey & mustard chicken slaw salad 84
  hot & sour chicken salad 34
  mango & peanut chicken salad 180
  piquant chicken & mixed pepper salad 124
  sesame chicken noodle salad 208
  smoked chicken, asparagus & blue cheese salad 44
  spicy chicken & fruit couscous salad 116
  spicy lemon chicken salad 130
  tandoori chicken & salad naans 74
  tomato salad 158
  Vietnamese chicken, herb & rice salad 128
  warm green chicken & rice salad 118
  yogurt chicken with greek salad 58
salami
  cacciatore chicken & salami ciabatta 210
  cacciatore-style chicken pasta 210
salsa, tomato
  balsamic chicken wraps 20
  chicken salsa wraps 20
  chicken tacos 68
salsa verde
  cold chicken with salsa verde 138
  poached chicken with spicy salsa verde 138
samosas, curried chicken 122
sandwiches
  broiled chicken & tomato sandwiches 78
  chicken, avocado & mustard sandwiches 156
  chicken & ham sandwiches 24
  chicken club sandwich 26
  chicken, orange & olive sandwiches 88
  herb chicken sandwiches 174
sauces
  creamy 212
  hot mustard 226
  lemon 80
  mustard 226
  nuoc cham 128
  red wine 216
  satay 166
sesame seeds
  sesame chicken & noodles 208
  sesame chicken noodle salad 208
shrimp
  chicken & shrimp spring rolls 100
  chicken, shrimp & lemon grass stir-fry 120
  Thai-style chicken patties 120
skewers see also kebabs
  green chicken skewers 118
  lemon & parsley chicken skewers 170
  lemon, mint & chicken skewers 40
  piquant chicken brochettes 124
  spicy chicken & mango skewers 150
  tandoori chicken skewers 74
  yogurt chicken with greek salad 58
snow peas
  spicy vietnamese chicken 142
soup
  chic   chicken & apple soup in a mug 28
  ken, eggplant & tomato soup 86
  chicken, mushroom & red wine soup 216
  chicken noodle broth 110
  chicken noodle soup 172
  ginger chicken soup 30
  hot & sour chicken soup 34
  Moroccan chicken & bean soup 98
  quick chicken & apple soup 28
  spicy chicken & rosemary soup 112
  Vietnamese chicken soup 142
soy sauce
  soy chicken & rice noodles 168
  soy noodles with chicken 168

spicy sticky soy-glazed chicken breasts 190
sticky soy-glazed drumsticks 190
spinach
chicken & goat cheese tarts 206
chicken, mushroom & spinach salad with spicy yogurt dressing 126
chicken, spinach & goat cheese tarts 206
spicy chicken crepes 126
yogurt chicken & spinach ciabatta 58
spring rolls, chicken & shrimp 100
star anise
spicy Vietnamese chicken 142
stews
chicken & apricot stew 82
Moroccan fruity chicken stew 98
spiced chicken stew 130
stir-fries
chicken & Asian vegetable stir-fry 96
chicken & vegetable stir-fry 96
chicken, shrimp & lemon grass stir-fry 120
quick sweet chili chicken stir-fry 90
soy noodles with chicken 168
stir-fried lemon chicken 192

sweet chili chicken stir-fry 90
sweet potatoes
mild & creamy chicken curry 92

tacos, chicken 68
tandoori paste
tandoori chicken & salad naans 74
tandoori chicken pita pockets 36
tandoori chicken skewers 74
tandoori chicken wings with raita 36
tarts see also pastries; pies
chicken & goat cheese tarts 206
chicken, spinach & goat cheese tarts 206
tomato salad 158
tortilla chips see nachos
tortillas
balsamic chicken wraps 20
chicken & apricot wraps 82
chicken, ham & cheese packages 184
chicken quesadillas 18
chicken salad wraps 26
chicken salsa wraps 20
Chinese chicken wraps 76
ginger chicken wraps 30
spicy chicken & feta rolls 220

vegetables
chicken & Asian vegetable stir-fry 96
chicken & shrimp spring rolls 100
chicken & vegetable satay 166
chicken & vegetable stir-fry 96
curried chicken samosas 122
curried chicken with vegetable rice 94
pan-fried chicken with roasted vegetables 228
quick sweet chili chicken stir-fry 90
roasted chicken & vegetables 228
sweet & spicy chicken noodles 132

water chestnuts
sweet chili chicken stir-fry 90
wraps see chapatis; tortillas

yogurt
chicken koftas 106
yogurt chicken & spinach ciabatta 58
tandoori chicken wings with raita 36
yogurt & harissa chicken kebabs 134
yogurt chicken with greek salad 58

zucchini
chicken & zucchini kebabs 38
chicken, bacon & zucchini baguettes 38
creamy chicken pasta 186

acknowledgments

Commissioning editor: Eleanor Maxfield
Designer: Tracy Killick
Editor: Alex Stetter
Assistant production manager: Caroline Alberti

Photography: Octopus Publishing Group Stephen Conroy
52–53, 108–109, 165, 181, 195, 201; Will Heap 1, 4–5,
7, 8, 29, 113, 115, 117, 119, 121, 125, 127, 129, 131, 133,
137, 139, 141, 143, 149, 151, 153, 175, 193, 211, 219,
221, 229, 231; Lis Parsons 2–3, 6, 9, 10–11, 13, 15, 17, 19,
21, 23, 25, 31, 33, 39, 41, 43, 45, 47, 49, 51, 55, 57, 59, 61,
63, 65, 69, 71, 73, 75, 77, 79, 81, 83, 85, 87, 89, 91, 93, 95,
97, 99, 101, 103, 105, 107, 123, 135, 145, 147, 154–155,
159, 163, 171, 179, 183, 187, 191, 204–205, 207, 217, 227;
William Reavell 35, 37, 111, 161, 177, 209; Craig Robertson
213, 223, 233; William Shaw 27, 67, 157, 167, 169, 173, 185,
189, 197, 199, 203, 215, 225.